The War on Critical Race Theory

The War on
Critical Race Theory

Or, the Remaking of Racism

DAVID THEO GOLDBERG

polity

Copyright © David Theo Goldberg 2023

The right of David Theo Goldberg to be identified as Author of this Work has been
asserted in accordance with the UK Copyright, Designs and Patents Act 1988.

First published in 2023 by Polity Press

Polity Press
65 Bridge Street
Cambridge CB2 1UR, UK

Polity Press
111 River Street
Hoboken, NJ 07030, USA

ISBN-13: 978-1-5095-5853-7 (hardback)
ISBN-13: 978-1-5095-5854-4 (paperback)

A catalogue record for this book is available from the British Library.

Library of Congress Control Number: 2022949654

Typeset in 11 on 14pt Warnock Pro
by Cheshire Typesetting Ltd, Cuddington, Cheshire
Printed and bound in Great Britain by CPI Group (UK) Ltd, Croydon

The publisher has used its best endeavors to ensure that the URLs for external
websites referred to in this book are correct and active at the time of going to
press. However, the publisher has no responsibility for the websites and can
make no guarantee that a site will remain live or that the content is or will remain
appropriate.

Every effort has been made to trace all copyright holders, but if any have been
overlooked the publisher will be pleased to include any necessary credits in any
subsequent reprint or edition.

For further information on Polity, visit our website:
politybooks.com

Contents

A Note on Acronyms

CRT   Critical Race Theory

CRT 1.0 the originally formulated legal Critical Race Theory

"CRT"   occasionally used to flag as wholly fabricated the conception of CRT projected by its strident critics

CRS   the broader field of Critical Race Studies

CLS   Critical Legal Studies

Preface

I was attending graduate school in New York City in the early 1980s as scholarly discussions of race and racism were ramping up. The body of work that came in the late 1980s to be identified as Critical Race Theory (CRT) was a burgeoning feature of these debates across the humanities and social sciences, though little noticed outside the academy.

The notable analytic Marxist philosopher Gerald Cohen came to my graduate school to talk about his work. At the reception he inquired what I was working on. "The philosophical foundations of racism," I responded. "You mean there are any?", he asked skeptically. "You will have to read my work," I countered. That was the sum of the skirmish as he turned to others to discuss what he clearly considered more serious philosophical matters.

Fast forward to late 2020, and Cohen's skepticism has assumed far more volatile consideration. CRT has been targeted as the threat of our time, the cultural equivalent of terrorism. So much so that critics in countries other than the U.S. had taken up the shrill cry. Having devoted a good part of my published scholarship to issues of race and racism since my graduate training, partly in conversation with the legal analysis of race, I was somewhat bemused by this turn. I could recognize little if anything of CRT or indeed of the body of critical work on racism with which I had long been engaged in what was so fast being taken up in the public sphere as the new target of the cultural wars. So, I was moved by mid-2021 to publish a couple of publicly oriented articles questioning what was at work in this new political turn.[1]

By the late Summer through early Fall of 2021, the excitement seemed to have dissipated, the rush run its course. But then the political season ramped up, most notably with a contested gubernatorial campaign in the state of Virginia. The battle cry aimed at CRT was clearly producing high-octane political outcomes. I took the call to build on the earlier articles and write a book on the new racially driven war games. *The War on Critical Race Theory* is the offering on order. My focus is on the targets and aims, the claims and concerns, in short, the politics at play in this manufactured set of campaigns.

This conception of CRT has been under fierce attack since late 2020. How, then, have the conservative criticisms branded the body of critical work on race and racism in ways pretty much completely remaking their terms of engagement and critique? In his robust defense of Critical Race Theory, Victor Ray has emphasized that ". . . [T]aking these [anti-CRT] attacks seriously means not attempting to directly refute or debunk many of the lies about critical race theory spread by bad-faith actors."[2] I appreciate Ray's concern: expanding coverage of the Klan in the 1920s directly increased its membership.

However, by contrast, I think it crucial for both a well-informed public and its political representation to understand the stakes in play, what anti-CRT proponents are saying and seeking to do. In *Policing the Crisis*, Stuart Hall and his colleagues famously traced the manufacture of the mainstream moral panic of "mugging" in mid-1970s Britain and the political uses to which it was put. They did not shy from spelling out in detail what the drivers of the fiction were expressing.

In 1981, Martin Barker similarly took on sociobiology's politics of exclusion, offering a sustained critical account of the ways conservative British politicians and public commentators were mobilizing biological accounts of cultural differences to rationalize the repatriation of recent migrants. I take inspiration here from their accounts.[3]

My principal aim is a sustained critical analysis of the attacks on CRT to assess both the standing of their claims and the political goals being pursued in their name. What frames of understanding regarding race and racism, as a consequence, are the conservative CRT critics concerned to have dominate the public sphere, policy, and action, in the U.S. and, with its partners, in Europe and those former colonies where whites fear their hold on cultural and political power slipping?

1

What's Going On?

Critical Race Theory (CRT) sits solidly atop the conservative hit list.

Since the election cycle evicting Donald Trump from the Oval Office, attacks on "Critical Race Theory" and defenses against them have spiraled. The vehemence, frequency, and venom, even the content of the attacks, have differed little from one to another. To the uninitiated, critical and defensive statements regarding CRT have sounded like refrains from competing songs in the busy jukebox of ideas. Death metal trying to drown out the blues.

U.S. Senator Tom Cotton, Republican of Arkansas, introduced a bill to the U.S. Senate in March 2021 seeking to ban the teaching of CRT in the military. He charged that it is "racist." He also wanted all Senate committees to review President Biden's nominations for general administrative positions for what they think about CRT. Florida Governor Ron DeSantis banned CRT from being covered in Florida's public schools for "teaching kids to hate their country and to hate each other." Republican majority lawmakers in the state of Idaho prohibited the use of state funding for student "social justice" activities of any kind at public universities. They also threatened to withhold funding earmarked for "social justice programming and critical race theory." Tennessee outlawed educators teaching that "an individual, by virtue of the individual's race or sex, is inherently privileged, racist, sexist, or oppressive, whether consciously or subconsciously." Similarly, Iowa has outlawed educators teaching that Iowa or the U.S. is systemically racist.

Texas is requiring the teaching of "multiple perspectives" or "opposing views" on "widely debated and currently controversial issues." The law is meant to dampen the teaching of "Critical Race Theory." Its vague wording has raised awkward concerns about whether "multiple perspectives" are required regarding inherent evils like slavery and the Holocaust and, if so, what that would look like. A similar bill in Wyoming failed to receive the requisite votes to pass after a Jewish lawmaker spoke out strongly against it, drawing connections between indigenous decimation, slavery, and the Holocaust.

Lawmakers in over thirty-five states have emulated or introduced laws restricting the use or teaching of "CRT." In September 2021, the Republican-dominated legislature in Wisconsin passed legislation to ban any teaching about "critical race theory," "race," and gender" in Wisconsin schools. They appended a list of nearly ninety outlawed terms. The list predictably included notions like "woke," "whiteness," "white supremacy," "structural bias," "structural racism," "systemic bias," "systemic racism," multicultural," "equity," and "intersection" (regarding the latter, driving instructors beware). But also "cultural proficiency," "land acknowledgment," "social justice," and "normativity." While unlikely to be signed into law by the Democratic Governor, a former school superintendent, the effort was designed to place teachers on notice that they are being profiled. Their Republican counterparts in the U.S. Congress introduced a bill to amend the 1964 Civil Rights Act to make it illegal to "us(e) critical race theory or critical race pedagogy in any program or activity receiving Federal financial assistance."

Similar attacks were afoot abroad. In Britain a government minister declared in October 2020 in a House debate that the government was "unequivocally against" the concept, even though official records show that the phrase "critical race theory" had never previously been uttered in the House of Commons.

An assistant attorney general in Australia proclaimed that an anti-racism program should not be funded because "taxpayer funds" were being used "to promote critical race theory." In South Africa, Helen Zille, the former Mayor of Cape Town and leader of the Democratic Alliance political party, has attacked CRT as "an academic fig leaf" to "justify legally codified racism." "Critical Race Theory" apparently has taken some flight. Obscurity has given way to a globally mobilized counter-offensive.

These criticisms have placed proponents of Critical Race Theory on the defensive. In the face of the conservative rallying cry at the political barricades, CRT defenders have resorted to pointing out that important distinctions are collapsed, meanings distorted, examples decontextualized. The civility of scholarly defenses has been pitted against the loudspeakers of strident political invective.

Until September 2020, almost only college law professors, social scientists, and humanists had paid even the vaguest attention to Critical Race Theory. Google searches for CRT surged in June 2021 after Florida restricted its teaching in public schools. And it outstripped again the search for "Black Lives Matter" (BLM) in November when Virginia elected Glen Youngkin as Governor, his opposition to CRT in Virginia schools perhaps making the significant difference in the vote. The shift in interest from BLM following the George Floyd murder to CRT a year later has tracked the tensions at play in racial politics.

The past half decade has witnessed profound unsettlements. Autocratic rulers have proliferated. How we work, and increasingly also where, has shifted dramatically. There's a growing sense that everything about our lives and relations is instantaneously available, that the private is in fact public. The pandemic deepened the sensed loss of control: over life's conditions, the availability of everything from basic food products to housing, computers, automobiles, even schooling. One's future seems less secure, more unsure. Even one's own reactions in ordinary circumstances have faltered. Everyday anger has proliferated, in stores, on flights, in the home. The growing anxiety over the effects of climate change have only exacerbated this loss of predictability. Disquiet has heightened, growing dread the palpable sense of our time.[1] The tensions over CRT reflect these broader social concerns.

*

What, or who, in the face of all of this, exactly shifted public perception, if not knowledge, regarding Critical Race Theory? Why has the anxiety, at least in part, assumed CRT as a palpable object?

Donald Trump, of all people. He had given no inkling about intellectual interest in a publicly obscure academic legal theory. In 2019, chatter on right-wing social media targeting the 1619 Project began to grow.[2] "CRT" became its dismissive branding. On September 2, 2020, President Trump happened to be slumped before a television in the White House. He was watching, of all programs, Tucker Carlson Tonight on Fox News. Perhaps he was looking for an ideological weapon to advance his Presidential election battle that November. Carlson was interviewing Christopher Rufo, little recognized at the time. Rufo was railing against "Critical Race Theory" as the new "default ideology" of the Federal Government, pervading its every institution. He had come to Carlson's notice by earlier appearances on Laura Ingraham's Fox show, followed by radio interviews with Rush Limbaugh and Glen Beck (reaching over 25 million people combined). With Carlson, Rufo called on the President to issue an immediate Executive Order to "stamp out" this "destructive, divisive . . . cult of indoctrination." In the name of canceling "cancel culture," Critical Race Theory unceremoniously had to be whited out.

Trump sat up. Rufo was invited to the White House. Three weeks later President Trump issued an Executive Order prohibiting all government agencies and contractors from providing employee training on any subjects related to race and gender. The Executive Order 13950 was officially established to "Combat Racial and Sex Stereotyping." It was dubbed the "Critical Race Theory EO."[3]

President Biden took office on January 20, 2021, and promptly rescinded Trump's regulation. But the radical public campaign to cancel "Critical Race Theory" was just ramping up, reaching the point of a veritable political panic. Like their moral counterpart, political panics are composed and orchestrated, their diffusion curated. The driving questions, then, are what exactly is the target, why, and why now? What is Critical Race Theory, and what do Rufo, his partners, and followers think it is? What organizations are driving these attacks, and who are acting on their behalf? What profile has CRT's critics fashioned about it, and what are their intended outcomes? In short, what are the politics in play regarding the fight against CRT?

Critical Race Theory has come under attack most furiously in the United States. French President Emmanuel Macron was right in one extended sense when he castigated the importation of "certain social science theories" from "American universities." The terms of rejection elsewhere are derivative of those formulated and fashioned in the U.S., and far less in scope and force. I focus in this book principally on the American battles over CRT. But I will also reference ways in which conservative critics elsewhere, in Europe especially, look to advance related concerns and claims.

Questions abound. Do the criticisms targeting Critical Race Theory represent a legitimate line of concern about youths' understanding of American life, past and present, and so of their futures? Or does CRT serve for our time much as "communism" was made to do for the 1940s and 1950s? Has CRT been so radically refashioned to serve as conservatives' political piñata, a convenient public flogging doll for self-serving political purpose no matter the political and personal costs to some destroyed lives and careers as a consequence?

Race and racism function as touchstones, historically and politically, for the state of the nation. They reflect thinking about what the country has been, where it is of late, and where we take ourselves collectively to be headed. This was certainly the case with the Civil War and the Civil Rights Movement. And it remains with us, if in renewed terms. The concepts, both in application and denial, reflect and register the contested ideals: of who fully belong to the national community, and what progress is being made to realize full belonging for all social groups.

Proponents of CRT and its vocal critics in the U.S. cannot both be right: about American history and memory, about the nature of racism as only an individual expression or as a key assessment of dominant social structure, and about the society's racial future. Who are the people and organizations headlining these attacks against CRT, and what do the proponents and practitioners of Critical Race Theory take it to stand for (Part I)? What do CRT's critics actually think it is that they are attacking and why do they think there is a need (Part II)? What is this sustained crusade mounted against CRT since late 2020 seeking to do? Is it undertaking to reclaim political power by using race once again as an instrument of division and control, by redefining its terms? What are the envisioned impacts of these attacks, but also the counters and challenges to them (Part III)?

The targeting of CRT has become especially strident. How cogent are the arguments being hurled at CRT, or are the public being "gaslighted"? Who, if anyone, is playing whom?

Are we witnessing in real time the elaboration of a new form of racism, building on while going beyond the old? If so, how, to what purpose, what ends and effects? "What's going on?", Marvin Gaye asked poignantly in 1971. That question remains as pressing as ever.

Part I

Principles and Principals

2

The Headliners

From late 2020, a new act seemed to come out of nowhere, taking strident aim at Critical Race Theory. Christopher Rufo has proved the frontman, spitting out the lyrics.

Rufo brandishes the anti-CRT microphone, the poster-boy for the attacks. He has set the terms. Pretty much all the subsequent conservative criticism has taken its cue from his framing and formulation. But he is not alone, fronting a band of political provocateurs whose collective orchestration has ignited the furious contempt of the singalong crowd. In this chapter I identify Rufo's principal band members, the headliners sourcing, funding, and circulating the charges.

Obsessed with the notion of Critical Race Theory, RealChrisRufo⚔, as he brands himself, crossed sword emoji for effect, projects himself as the brilliant lone crusader brandishing his magic sabres.[1] Donald Trump provided the initiative with a national platform. But, arguably, it was the Heritage Foundation that appears actually to have launched it. A lone ranger doesn't so readily make Fox News star turns, Limbaugh or Beck, without a calling card. Numerous Heritage agents, or agents provocateur, quickly jumped to the task. Jonathan Butcher and Mike Gonzalez were the other two who joined

Rufo for the work. Gonzalez had published a book targeting identity politics. It centered terms that Rufo half a year later would initially mobilize to attack CRT.[2] Butcher and Gonzalez are employed at Heritage, while Rufo held affiliate status at the Foundation when the initiative took off in late 2020.

Butcher, Gonzalez, and Rufo, separately or in some combination, have composed approximately 70 percent of the dismissive articles on CRT appearing on the Heritage Foundation website. Now Director of the Manhattan Institute's Critical Race Theory initiative and a contributing editor of their *City Journal*, Rufo has published approximately thirty articles for them since Trump's Executive Order, close to all of that platform's contributions on the subject. The initial articles tended to outline contestable claims about CRT's history and central principles, widely adopted subsequently by conservative critics. Since late 2021 their publications have tended to focus on surfacing expressions, programs, or events they seek to decry and dismiss as CRT.

Collectively, the three anointed by Heritage as "CRT afficionados" have impeccable conservative credentials, having worked for or with the last two Republican administrations, and for their leading think tanks, foundations, and institutes. None of the Heritage men, however, are trained as lawyers, or indeed in any field specializing in studies of race. To their credit they have picked up a version of CRT along the way. Their untrained eyes seem to be seeing what the trained ones have not (intended), reconfirming the sighted UFO in consultation with each other. The question is whether the result has been the composition of something hardly resembling the real thing.

Christopher Rufo, though, is the one who has gained the most traction from targeting CRT. He seems to have found his niche as a leading race ideologue and media influencer for the right. He has parlayed this of late into founding and directing a "public policy research center." The name "Battlefront" extends his self-identity as the crusader, leading the brigade into the culture war that the right is waging. Being the crusade's voice is quite literally his fulltime employment, perhaps even, like a typecast Hollywood actor, his employability. While pronouncing that "CRT is everywhere," he is the one swinging away repeatedly on Fox News, where Trump saw him interviewed and immediately gave Rufo a national bullhorn. (Across 2021, Fox News mentioned CRT/Critical Race Theory 4,500 times; 700 mentions in June alone or pretty much every two minutes throughout the month.) If his Twitter account is anything to go by, Rufo seems overwhelmingly obsessed with the subject. Rufo is the CRT critic who has contributed most to national outlets like *USA Today*, been profiled in the *Washington Post*, the *New York Times*, the *New Yorker* . . . and on and on. It is less CRT that is everywhere than it is Rufo's contrived formulation of it.

Rufo became the Trumpeter of anti-anti-racist agitation. So much so that his Twitter handle, @realchrisrufo, is also his platform for personal fundraising. He has about 175,000 followers; though he blocked me for modestly pointing out to them some of his falsifications. In taking on the Trumpian mantle, make-believe is the name of the game. And, like the notorious propagandists from whom he clearly has drawn lessons, fabrication is at the heart of Rufo's real crusade, as I detail in Part II. He is well trained in this, after all. His principal employment while affiliated with Heritage and before moving over to the Manhattan Institute was with the Discovery Institute, notorious for its creationist and anti-evolution science denial.

*

The Heritage Foundation is among the most influential shapers of conservative thought and policy in the U.S. The Foundation appears to have designed a dual states-centered political strategy to support the right-wing resurrection and return to political power: a broadside on progressive anti-racism, which the attack on CRT has spear-headed; and the superficially neutral-looking voter suppression of people of color, the poor, and youth. The work to constrain voting[3] has been led, quietly, by Heritage Action (launched as a stand-alone legal action group by the Heritage Foundation in 2010). Heritage Action has developed a template for state voting restrictions, in some cases helping to write the proliferating state legislation in ways that have exemplified an action model for the attacks on CRT.[4] Today, a third focus could be added, the burgeoning attack on LGBTQ+ rights.

The principal funding underwriting the coordinated campaign against CRT has come from a small circle of billionaire sources. Initial funding derived from the Koch network, funneled through both the Heritage Foundation and Manhattan Institute. Despite continuing to provide funding, the Koch organization has since declared that CRT should not be banned or censored, in the spirit of its libertarian commitment to free expression. No one seems to have noticed. A nod and a wink.

An obscure family fund based in Boca Raton, Florida, the Thomas W. Smith Foundation, is sponsored by the hedge-fund manager whose name the Foundation bears.[5] It is run by James Piereson, who is also a fellow at the Manhattan Institute, of which Thomas Smith is a Trustee. Smith Foundation funds targeting CRT are likewise being run through Heritage and Manhattan.

The Concord Fund is a dark money group monetarily supporting conservative causes. It is fronted by the Judicial Crisis Network, best known for deep-pocket funding for voter restriction initiatives. Carrie Campbell Severino serves as the President of the Judicial Crisis Network. She clerked for Justice Clarence Thomas, with whom she remains close. Severino is active also with the Federalist Society and its well-heeled co-Chairman Leonard Leo. Leo was a key player in vetting Trump appointees to the federal judiciary and, especially, the Supreme Court. The Concord Fund aired advertisements in the tens of millions to generate public support for President

Trump's three ultra-conservative Supreme Court nominees. In the summer of 2021, the Concord Fund contributed "well over $1 million" targeting for elimination racial justice teaching in K-12 curricula.[6] This further highlights the coordinated campaign linking the line of attacks on CRT to the efforts on voting barriers.

So, it is in fact a tight circle of critics and funders that has composed the campaign against CRT. The Manhattan Institute and its *City Journal* is one.[7] The Heritage Foundation has installed a "Critical Race Theory Legislation Tracker," keeping a running tab on state and federal legislation to curtail or outright ban CRT and its teaching.[8] The Leadership Institute has provided decades-long coordination of attacks on progressive critical thought. It has trained legions of young activists and political leaders, from Mike Pence to Mitch McConnell, Grover Norquist to Ralph Reed. The number includes Project Veritas's James O'Keefe, renowned as the right-wing "gotcha" activist for misleadingly editing videos to destroy progressive politicians and academics. The Leadership Institute teaches its students that "CRT," at least in the version shaped by Rufo, is committed to "undermining social and governmental norms."

Given the popularity in some circles of the attacks on CRT, these organizations have all been quick to fundraise explicitly off this line of commitments. They're all lining up to monetize "leadership" in solely self-advancing ways.

It should come as no surprise, too, that Campus Reform and Turning Point USA have joined the attacks. Both advocate for politically conservative values at schools, colleges, and universities, and see CRT as the sort of liberalism on campus they are committed to eradicating. They weaponize the criticisms of CRT to spy on faculty and students across the country they take to be too liberal – too critical-race inclined – for the national good. Freedom of expression is constrained for all but those shouting agreement with them. The more intellectually inclined organs, *National Review* and the Claremont Institute's

American Mind, unsurprisingly also get in on the act, publishing articles rehashing the Rufo-esque talking points.

*

The contemporary influence of Rufo on anti-CRT rhetorical expression and practice has been ubiquitous. The history of CRT that its strident critics have adopted pretty much verbatim is the one Rufo has laid out for them. The dominant terms supposedly defining CRT are those he has mostly provided in videos, publications, and talks. As too are the terms of critical dismissal – "Marxist," "equity," "woke," "cancel culture," and the like – adapted to this instance from more general rejection of "liberal" culture by the right. Florida's Governor DeSantis predicated his 2022 re-election and possibly 2024 Presidential campaigns on "fight[ing] the woke in schools . . . and in businesses." The examples of nefarious CRT application rampantly invoked, whether in schools, colleges, workplaces, or government agencies, are largely the ones Rufo has licensed himself to identify.

Now, Rufo claims repeatedly to have "conducted a study" from which he then cites examples widely taken up by others. This catchphrase provides a scholarly ring to the standard Trumpian recourse to "people are telling me . . ." when he is looking to say whatever he wants. No details of the study are ever provided, no citations, no context. The examples tend to be radically decontextualized, leaving out key details, or may have been ideas under discussion and never implemented, as Rufo alleges. And the practices of institutional and individual surveillance generally circulated by CRT critics are those Rufo has widely promoted.

Given the debt Rufo and Trump owe each other, it would not be so far-fetched to name the ideology that has emerged from this partnership "Trufism," its followers "Trufers." Trufism is Rufo's rant gone national. Trump without Rufo would not have alighted on CRT as political fuel; Rufo without Trump would not have his national soapbox. Rufo gave Trump's racial crassness a veneer behind which his supporters could nod their support: the Central Park Five's supposed guilt even after complete judicial exoneration; Obama birtherism; all Mexican migrants as "rapists" and "murderers"; refusing immigration from "shithole countries"; the Haitian migrants gathering at the Mexican border "probably having AIDS"; the adoption of "America First," a 1920s Ku Klux Klan emblem, as his political brand; his awkward remarks and a campaign flyer about Jews and money; and an easy embrace of the white right's "great replacement" anxieties. The romance with Trump, on the other hand, gave Rufo a bully pulpit, amplified on Fox News and social media like Twitter and YouTube.

I will thus name "Trufism" this marriage of Trump and Rufo, Trumpism and Rufoism. It includes, as we will see, the completely make-believe "Marxist" history Rufo develops of CRT's supposed influences, sources, and developments accompanied by the equally fabricated characterizations he suggests about the doctrine (the band led by Rufo offers virtually no arguments). Trufism, in short, is nothing else than a bald set of make-believe assertions made an ideology. And "Trufers" are those who take them up, putting them to work in various contexts and applications. What Trufism adds to political debate is what Trump's floundering media platform Truth Social contributes to politics. The aim of both is to blow up social arrangements over which they exercise little if any control, replacing them with invented "truths" designed for self-advancement. Trufism licenses itself to take total liberties with the truth. It is to reliable accuracy as Truth Social has proved to dependability.

*

Legions of people showing up to school-board meetings and protests have been activated by Rufo's pronouncements and public appearances, from Virginia and Tennessee to Florida and Texas, Wisconsin and Arizona. In June 2021, following the George Floyd murder and protests, a school-board meeting in a wealthy Virginia suburb erupted when an audience of all white parents and outside agitators accused the board of mandating the teaching to students of CRT, and in its name the history of American structural and systemic racism. The gathering got so heated – abusive language rose above the din, arms flailed – that the board abandoned the meeting. Police intervened to disperse the crowd, arresting two attendees for failing to comply. Similar eruptions at such meetings have occurred around the country.

Taking their lead and language from Rufo, protestors have mobilized for over two-hundred school-board recall efforts in eighty districts, the highest number on record.[9] But, even more influentially, there are organizations that have adopted Rufo's thinking on CRT and advanced the impact of his interventions. These include the Center for Renewing America/Citizens for American Renewal, the Nevada Family Alliance, the Legal Insurrection Foundation and its spin off the Critical Race Theory Education Project. There are a handful of politicians, too, joining the chorus in especially vocal ways: Senators Tom Cotton of Arkansas, Ted Cruz of Texas, and Josh Hawley of Missouri; Governors Ron DeSantis of Florida, Greg Abbott of Texas, and Kristi Noem of South Dakota. That local Republican state legislators, like Virginia's Neil Freitas, are choir members too makes further evident the calculation of political capital in play.[10] All told, though, the second ring circling the core is likewise a small group beating the drums to which the protest crowds and less visible politicians are then chanting in call and response.

Citizens for Renewing America is a Trump-inspired organization.[11] Its founding President, Russel Vought, served in the Trump administration as Deputy Director and then, more briefly, as Director of the Office of Management and Budget. Vought has pronounced that "Muslims do not simply have a deficient theology. They do not know God because they have rejected Jesus Christ his Son, and they stand condemned."

Vought has also offered up repeatedly contested data. The organization is committed, according to its website, to providing "the ideological ammunition to sustain Trump's political movement after his departure from the White House."

In this spirit, Citizens for Renewing America offers a "Toolkit for Combatting Critical Race Theory."[12] In purporting to define CRT, its definitions and reasoning are so overgeneralized, under-theorized, and unreferenced that pretty much anything critical of racism fits. But perhaps that's the point. The initiative's listed staff appear to be all white, a telling indication of what "renewing America" and who is effecting it amount to. The organization offers "model schoolboard language to prohibit CRT" together with a "toolkit" to "combat CRT in your community,"[13] much as Heritage Action provides model legislation to suppress voting within states. The implication of these combined efforts, clearly, is that racial and religious diversity should be narrowed, along something like Trumpian lines.

The Nevada Family Alliance characterizes itself as a group advocating both in Nevada and nationally for parental rights and religious freedom. A fierce critic of CRT,[14] the Alliance has been a leading voice in advocating for teachers to wear body cameras to ensure they are not teaching some ill-defined conception of "critical race theory." Standing on freedom, this push mimics the Chinese government's experiment with cameras in school classrooms to monitor in real time children's cognitive and emotional responses to the lessons being offered them by their teachers.

As if body cameras do not suffice for tracking, the Legal Insurrection Foundation (LIF) was started by a Cornell law professor, William A. Jacobson, and two younger activists, Anne Segal and Martha Wollick. It is telling that before their website actually reveals what the Foundation exists to do, they ask readers to donate money to them, at least two or three times over. Give them your money and they will tell you who they are and what they may use it for! A few page clicks in they admit to having a "non-exclusive focus" on the "intersectional left's" obsession at "the crossover of anti-capitalism and anti-Zionism."[15] In their minds these constitute "the driving forces behind current attacks on individual liberty, economic freedom, and freedom of speech."

While K-12 schools have been the principal critical focus of those trying to root out CRT, LIF targets colleges and universities for tracking too. They have spun off a website, Critical Race Training in Education.[16] Drawing calculatingly on the Rufoistic misreadings – as a law professor at a notable law school, Jacobson surely should know better – this project monitors and reports on "more than 300 colleges and universities" nationwide for their training in "critical race theory" and anti-racism. Individual liberty apparently does not include academic freedom.

Jacobson has simply applied to monitor CRT by the censorious and insidious surveillance tactics honed by David Horowitz and his "Freedom Center." Horowitz, you may recall, has published an annual list of "the 100 most dangerous academics in America," all intellectuals left of center and many critical of Israeli treatment of Palestinians. Yet ideological inflation has no bounds, as LIF is also listing courses in *critical theory*, with no focus on racism. The overarching aim seems to be to warn "parents" away from sending their children to such institutions, including Jacobson's own, and by implication to pressure the institutions to end CRT-related courses. Cancel culture without the courage of its convictions.

Others have jumped on this bandwagon too. Many of the most notable conservative Black scholars in the U.S. have gathered under the title "1776 Unites." The group was founded by Robert Woodson to counter the 1619 Project. Its engagement has become more animated, wading into the swamp of anti-CRT activism. 1776 Unites issued an open letter advocating that school boards throughout the country should adopt their group's curriculum in place of CRT's (by the latter they seem to imply the curriculum of the 1619 Project), focusing on "the ideals of the founding fathers." Their curriculum collects historical stories illustrating "what is best in our national character and what our freedom makes possible even in the most difficult circumstances." The emphasis on individual agency "celebrate[s] Black excellence, reject[s] victimhood culture, and showcase[s] African-Americans who have prospered by embracing America's founding ideals."[17]

The Chinese American Citizens Alliance Greater New York (CACAGNY) has added its name to this anti-CRT activism. The group had filed an amicus brief in the Supreme Court case challenging purported discrimination by Harvard University against Asian-American student applicants (as I show later, the attacks on affirmative action have been folded into those on CRT). In the first half of 2021, thick hand-addressed envelopes with no return address were mailed out to university faculty across the U.S. It is unclear whether the materials were mailed directly by CACAGNY, or made available to supporters by them to be used as the latter found fit. The contents included an eight-page screed denouncing CRT as "hateful fraud." The documents echoed essays sponsored by the Heritage Foundation calling CRT "the new intolerance" and "the rejection of the underpinnings of Western civilization."[18] The materials suggest a more coordinated, if broadly distributed campaign than many seem to have realized.

Prominent right-wing influencers such as Mark R. Levin and David Horowitz have jumped on the blaring bandwagon too. Levin's *American Marxism* devotes a lengthy chapter to CRT, which I discuss at greater length at points in Part II. David Horowitz has published a book attacking the media for ascribing racial characterization to events garnering great public attention like police killings – when, he pronounces, such charges are overwhelmingly "a racial hoax."[19] His criticism, it seems, is that where there cannot be shown to be individual racial intent no racism exists. If you cannot show intent after the fact somehow racism didn't exist before the fact or in the act. Trufers like Horowitz demonstrate imperviousness as they commonly commit fallacies of reasoning. Warming up the crowd for the main act is all that matters.

Even theologians are getting in on the act. Voddie Baucham is an African-American dean of a seminary in Zambia, who grew up in Watts, Los Angeles. Baucham attributes to CRT that it uniquely fashions "racism" as its own idol of "Original Sin," in the process making impossible any hope of "forgiveness."[20] Similarly, the radical religious group mentioned above, the Center for Renewing America, charges CRT with undertaking to crucify the basic American commitment that "all men are created equal, endowed by their Creator with unalienable rights to life, liberty, and the pursuit of happiness." A prompting concern of Critical Race Theory in fact was that, in too many instances from the outset of the Republic, America has failed to live up to this founding principle. By contrast, the attacks on CRT have fueled a Gospel of Colorblindness, as I discuss in Chapter 6 below.[21]

The message, it seems, is the massage, ideological as much as material. To assess whether criticisms being dismissively hurled by the Trufers at CRT take aim at the actual doctrine or have conjured a straw doll, a political piñata, for questionable political purpose, it is imperative to outline briefly CRT's actual history, what it in fact seeks to stand for, and its central concepts of analysis.

3

Critical Race Theory

It is obvious that the critical headliners identified in the previous chapter believe CRT to have fatal, and fatally dangerous, flaws. Before turning to what they take these flaws, failures, and fatal dangers to be, it would prove helpful to understand what the theory's founders actually understood it to be and why they saw any need for it.

What came to be called Critical Race Theory from the 1980s on is the mode of legal analysis that developed largely out of Harvard Law School. Let's call this CRT 1.0. There were two driving inspirations for the theory's development. The first, as almost all commentaries note, was a critical response to a theory popular in some quarters of the law academy in the mid-to-later 1970s, Critical Legal Studies (CLS). Influenced by Marxism, CLS argued that the structure of American law was designed to service and protect dominant class interests. Little recognized, though, is that CLS was taking sides in a deeper underlying discussion about the driving determinants of late twentieth-century social structure, especially in the West.

Almost never remarked is that there was a wider set of intellectual discussions at work underpinning this emergence of

CRT. By the later 1970s, a debate had broken out in the social sciences about whether class or race served as the dominant determining force in social structure. In 1967, the Kerner Commission had published a damning report about race in the U.S.[1] Commissioned by President Lyndon Johnson in the wake of the countrywide urban uprisings, the Kerner Report demonstrated with considerable data and detail the ways race had come to structure "two societies, separate and unequal" in the U.S. The picture it portrayed was of a deeply racially divided country. A decade later, in 1978, the notable African-American sociologist, William Julius Wilson, then at the University of Chicago, published *The Declining Significance of Race*.[2] The book set off a quite furious academic debate. Wilson argued that race had become a less impactful condition driving prospects in America, increasingly overridden by inequality and economic class concerns.

There were overlapping debates in other societies. Earlier in the 1970s, the race–class debate in South Africa dominated the social sciences. Marxist sociologists and historians had been arguing for some time that class formation was the driving condition of labor exploitation and social inequality, and that race was a rationalizing ideology – an epiphenomenon – undertaking to legitimate this deeper class foundation. Critics pushed back that class (alone) failed to explain the particularities and peculiarities of South Africa's apartheid social structure. Without recourse to race as a socially structuring condition, no satisfactory explanation could be provided as to why it was *Black* labor that was so deeply exploited. It was these critical sociologists and historians who coined the term "racial capitalism" to characterize South Africa's political economy at the time. Stuart Hall revealed patterns of segregation in Britain comparable to those in states more readily recognized for their structures of racial domination, fueled by the ways race and class weaved together in the society (what he called their "articulation").[3]

Scholars in the U.S. were quick to counter sociologist Wilson, demonstrating with copious data the overreach of his claims. Andrew Hacker's detailed updating of the Kerner Commission, from which he adopted his book's title, *Two Nations: Black and White*, left little doubt.[4] By the mid-1990s the lived experiences and prospects of Black and white citizens were as starkly at odds as they had ever been. Hacker, a thorough but hardly radical political scientist, collected in one place the revealing data that had surfaced through the 1980s and into the 1990s, showing a deepening of those divisions. Blacks and whites lived, schooled, worked, and socialized largely apart. As the revealing idiom has it, the most segregated place and time in America is church hour on Sundays.

In each of the national cases, whether in the U.S., Britain, or South Africa, it was not that class mattered only, or that race mattered more. It was that both did, contextually and interactively.

The second driving inspiration for the development of CRT 1.0, as accounts both attacking and supporting CRT all emphasize, was Derrick Bell's seminal work. After graduating from law school at the University of Pittsburgh, Bell worked for the civil rights division of the Justice Department. Asked to resign his membership in the NAACP because of potential conflicts of interest, he refused. Instead, he left the Justice Department, and in 1959 assumed a position under Thurgood Marshall at the NAACP Legal Defense Fund. His work there was devoted to desegregating schools. At the outset of the 1960s Bell joined USC's law school, before being hired by Harvard Law School toward the end of the decade. In 1971, he became the first Black law faculty member to receive tenure at Harvard. A decade later he assumed the deanship of law at the University of Oregon, before returning to Harvard in 1985. By 1990 he had become deeply disillusioned with Harvard Law's inability to hire any Black women faculty. Bell took unpaid leave in protest, spending the rest of his career as a visiting professor at NYU Law School.

While at Harvard, Bell sought to intervene in the debate about race and class. He was abidingly skeptical about racial progress in America. This critical skepticism centered on his concern that racisms were so embedded in America's legally protected structures that they might prove impossible to erase. Whites have long tended to resist race-specific programs to address structurally reproduced racial inequalities. So, the only way changes to this landscape of inequality could begin to be taken up with any chance for success in America, Bell realized, was by crafting universal policies that whites could support and from which they too would benefit. But, he saw clearly, these policies, in turn, tended invariably to entrench and extend the existing inequalities. For example, replacing affirmative action with race-neutral income-based college admissions programs has tended more readily to benefit whites, especially women, than Black applicants. These accordingly end up more deeply cementing campus racial homogeneity.

CRT 1.0 was forged by a diverse group of young legal scholars, many of whom were Bell's students at Harvard. They were concerned to offer a dynamic methodological account to resolve the driving theoretical tensions Bell helped to identify. The initiating group included Kimberlé Crenshaw, Patricia Williams, Mari Matsuda, Charles Ogletree, Charles Lawrence, Kendall Thomas, Neil Gotanda, Richard Delgado, Gary Peller, Cheryl Harris, Angela Harris, Gerald Torres, and others. All would go on to notable careers in American law schools.

If there is a single driving architect mobilizing generations of CRT contributors to keep developing the analysis and its generative applications, it would be Kimberlé Crenshaw. (Crenshaw has emphasized throughout that she is one among many, that the importance of the undertaking is precisely its multiple contributors and their intellectual interaction. CRT 1.0 is pointedly *not* Crenshawism.) She grew up in Canton,

Ohio, her parents active in desegregation efforts locally. She received her undergraduate education from Cornell, and her law degree from Harvard. Following an LLM degree from the University of Wisconsin, Crenshaw clerked for a Wisconsin Supreme Court judge. She holds endowed chairs in Law at both UCLA and Columbia University. At Columbia, she founded and directs the Center for Intersectionality and Social Policy Studies. At UCLA, she was among a small faculty group establishing the Law School certificate focus on Critical Race Studies (CRT 1.0), a flagship law school education program.

Independently, Crenshaw developed and directs the African American Policy Forum committed to "dismantling structural inequality." The Forum offers training and policy development to impact law and society in productive ways. Her work proved crucially important in drafting the equality clause of South Africa's post-apartheid Constitution, a key instrument since 1994 in seeking to mobilize legal equality in that country. Crenshaw has been a force in calling attention to police violence and brutality against Black women in the U.S. She was key in initiating the "Say Her Name" movement, proposing the moniker which has since taken hold. She recently joined with Janelle Monae for her widely circulated music video, "Say Her Name," protesting police brutality against Black women.

*

In its original legal iteration, CRT 1.0 emphasized the importance of attending to race in U.S. legal and court analysis. The legal analysts of 1.0 posed the questions: does race matter, and if so how? They found race to be *intersectionally* or interactively operative with other key social positionings such as class, gender, disability, and so on. CRT 1.0 formed an important and influential analytic lens for legally comprehending the perpetuation of racial and other hierarchical injustices through the institutional structure of the law. The aim has been to bring these institutionalizing mechanisms to light, and to develop tools to render social arrangements more racially equitable and just.

A robust scholarship in the social sciences and humanities emerged in the late 1970s and through the 1980s, focusing on race and racism. What prompted this outpouring of work was the challenge to explain why racisms continued to cleave the country so deeply despite the Civil Rights Act more than a decade earlier. CRT 1.0 focused on the ways law has helped to perpetuate racial inequalities that continued to benefit whites at the expense of Blacks, Latinos, Asians, and the indigenous. The broader human science research questioned the ongoing hold of historical racial arrangements, and the roles of political economy, social ordering, and culture in this perpetuation.

CRT 1.0's key conceptual commitments developed in conversation with this broader body of scholarship. This inter-disciplinary work was ideologically and politically diverse: there were liberal and Marxist inspired accounts, those with feminist commitments, and those methodologically underpinned by discourse analysis, Michel Foucault, and Max Weber.

New historical scholarship on global and American slav-ery began circulating widely in this period.[5] Historians of ideas showed racial thinking in the U.S. and Europe to be a product of nineteenth and early twentieth-century science.[6] Philosophers questioned whether race was a biological or social fact, something indelibly determining people's prospects, or a product of social design.[7] Sociologists challenged Wilson's eclipse of race by class, calling for a more integrative account.[8] Feminist scholarship became increasingly concerned with how race, class, and gender were deeply interlaced, in the past and present of racial thinking.[9] Cultural and literary theorists examined how race was woven into novels as expressions of everyday culture.[10] They examined how reading racially shaped ways of seeing and experiencing for readers. At the same time, the exclusive focus by analysts on the targets or "objects" of racism opened up to include analysis of the "agents" producing and benefitting from racial ideas. Whiteness studies was the outcome of this latter development.[11]

There is no reductive singularity or even coherence to this wide-ranging body of racial analysis, theoretically, methodologically, ideologically, or indeed politically. This was an exciting if sprawling set of innovative scholarship. Conferences, courses, and college curricula flourished. Journals were launched, publications in the field multiplied. No single view dominated. As with scholarship generally, some voices rose to the front. Schools of thought formed, were criticized, got revised or overtaken. Scholars who took race to be the key defining feature of people's life chances were in sustained critical conversation with Black politically conservative analysts and commentators, such as Thomas Sowell or Glen Loury. Like Wilson's more liberally centrist views, these commentators believed that race had ceased to be the principal determinant of social life. This range of contrasting and often contesting accounts is just how academic scholarship and public intellectual debates tend to work.

It is against the backdrop of this broader exchange that Critical Race Theory (CRT 1.0) took hold. It engaged with the driving academic and social debates of the day, while attending to legal and social challenges regarding ongoing racism, as Reagan's agenda of racial criminalization and retrenchment hardened. The wider field developed in conversation with CRT 1.0 in its original socio-legal formulation into what I characterize more generally as "critical race studies" (CRS). The impacts were considerable.

Law is woven more-or-less thickly through many of these themes and concerns, though far from exhausting them. So, it is worthwhile maintaining the distinction between CRT 1.0, the legal doctrine, and the broader field of Critical Race Studies, to see where they overlap and diverge. The burgeoning critical focus on race in the academic studies of education from the 1990s on in the U.S. and Britain, for example, was in fact conducted under the self-proclaimed banner of "Critical Race Theory," even though CRT 1.0 was not nearly as central to the educational debates as the outlawing of racial talk in schooling would now have it. While deploying some analytic concepts inherited from CRT 1.0, educational studies from the 1990s on in fact represented the broader scope of CRS.

The distinctions between these variations of critical racial analysis can be confusing. CRS and socio-legal CRT 1.0 are often taken together, sometimes by their proponents, but far more readily by the dismissive critics such as Christopher Rufo and his followers. Indeed, the latter have played on collapsing them. In their drive to dismiss all accounts critical of racism, the current vicious attacks misleadingly ignore any distinction between CRT 1.0 and CRS. In any case, the historical revisionism from these critics of CRT appears to be unconcerned with – and many were totally ignorant about – the broader historical context I have laid out here. For them, it is as if CRT 1.0 dropped mysteriously out of nowhere.

It bears pointing out here that a principal defining question of the social sciences since their formative inception not quite two centuries ago has focused on the explanatory contrast between *structure* and *agency*. Is the primary explanation of social life a matter of the way it is structured (at least in part by law), or the choices individuals make about their individual circumstances, the agency they exercise over their lives and those of others (or, of course, some interactive relation between the two)? This has marked social theorizing about race and racism at least from W.E.B. Du Bois's groundbreaking study of "The Philadelphia Negro" in 1897.[12] It also runs clear through the scholarship on race and class mentioned earlier. Seemingly without recognizing it, then, critics of CRT like Rufo are assuming a full-throated commitment in this formative debate. For them, in notable contrast to those committed to CRT 1.0 or CRS analysis, individual agency and not social structure is the sole driving cause of racism today. I will demonstrate this more fully in the chapters that follow.

*

In its original legal formulation, CRT 1.0 codified a set of key framing insights and concepts. These were drawn in part from participation in the broader debates shaping theoretical work on race and racism. They came to constitute the core CRT conceptual commitments in its analysis. CRT 1.0, then, tells a story about how race historically and through law has structured the U.S., and continues to do so. As we have come to learn with technology, v. 1.0 can sometimes offer much clearer, more reliable, and user-friendly service than later versions, despite all the additional bells and whistles the latter might add. So too with CRT 1.0. What follows is a summary of six core conceptual commitments through which CRT 1.0 formulates its account.

Racial Anti-Essentialism

First, CRT 1.0's understanding is that there is no biological basis to the concept of race. CRS shares this understanding with CRT 1.0. Race, in the language widely adopted, is a "social construction." It is an elastic social fiction, a "social fact" not a biological one. Race gets "concretized" as a concept, the malleability of which has enabled it to be used overwhelmingly and repeatedly at different times and places to define, fix in place, and disadvantage preconceived and maligned groups. The point of such disadvantaging is to advance and extend the advantage, currently more readily called "privilege," of those racially self-defined groups who have relative power. The elastic and malleable quality of race as concept and phenomenon entails that race, and the particular races it names, has no essential qualities other than those that powerful social groups tend to assign to them. The broader culture reinforces, circulates, and assumes the contrasts these powerful groups shape and assign. These ascribed characterizations include racial superiority and inferiority, differences and distinctions in habits, behavior, and patterns of reasoning.

Structural Racism

Furthermore, CRT 1.0 considers racism not as a series of discrete one-off aberrations or instances of breaking the rules of an otherwise civilized society, but rather structured into the ordinary experience of everyday life in modern states. It is deemed endemic, historically and enduringly, to social life, in America and elsewhere. The casual degrading remarks and structurally ordered inequalities are historically produced and socially embedded. They are then passed on as they also morph from one generation to another, in society after society. The strident Trufist attacks on CRT scoff at the ongoing existence of structural racism in the U.S., as I show in Chapter 5.

Racial Interests

The reproduction of racism, CRT argues, is driven in part by the overlapping interests that whites, as whites, are taken to share. It is on the basis of such shared interests that they may create policies and act to satisfy and extend those interests. That the interests overlap – they "converge," in CRT 1.0 language – does not mean that they are always identical. The interests are not necessarily uniform. They may be individual and subjective, or pertain to a group as a group. At any time or on any issue not all whites need share an interest. Workers may best be served by acting together, say striking, to secure higher wages. But (most) white workers may think their other privileges, say preferential promotion, would be better secured by excluding Black workers, not striking, and throwing in their lot with their white supervisors or employers. In 1943, as one example among many, thousands of white Detroit workers struck for a week against Packard Motors for hiring two Black workers.[13] They were prepared to forego a quarter of their monthly salary in the short term to restrict competition driving down wages in the longer term.

So, people of different racial backgrounds may share interests, for example, in mutual economic betterment, or in resisting racism. It follows that only when cross-racial interests converge, racial justice in the circumstances might be achievable. But the more central and pressing the interests to whites – maintaining power, for instance – the more likely, CRT argues, most will act as a group to uphold and extend them at the cost of curtailing or killing the possibility of realizing more general interests in common with racial others. The attacks on CRT in American schools appear to bear this out quite clearly. This repeated resort to racial interests by white parents when it came to integrating schools was also one of the sources of Derrick Bell's intentionally provocative racial skepticism, mentioned earlier. By the time he took leave of Harvard, Bell had grown wary of whites' passive-aggressive resistance to school integration. He mused aloud whether Black children might fare better, psychologically and educationally, in well-resourced segregated schools.

Racisms

The racism in one place and time is related if not (fully) reducible and identical to racism in other places and states, and reinforced by it. Hence the repeated charge in different times and places of a "new racism," a racism taking on new features and expressions. There is, accordingly, not just a single racism but racisms overlapping and not always narrowly reducible one to another. They are members of a common set, sharing the commonality of "racism," by way of their family resemblances. From the 1960s on, these racisms increasingly came to be reinforced by a dominant ideology, legally and socially, of "colorblindness." By the 1990s this anti-liberal commitment was identified by critical scholars as "racism without race or racists."[14] From the outset CRT has forged a critical analysis of the role "colorblindness" has played across the past hundred-and-twenty-five years of American socio-legal history. I will return to this notion of colorblindness, especially in Chapter 6.

Intersectionality

Legal CRT 1.0 showed, quite definitively, not only that class and race both mattered in positioning people socially. They mattered, CRT suggested, in ways interactively and reinforcing their effects. This interactive social positioning by race, class, and other such orderings including most notably gender, the key CRT 1.0 theorist Kimberlé Crenshaw, inspired by the Combahee River Collective's conception in 1977, famously popularized as "intersectionality."

People are socially positioned in terms of power and access, benefits and lacks, not just by their class belonging. They are positioned also by their racial background and inheritance, their gender, their (perceived) physical and cognitive capacities, and so on, and by the interaction of these positionings. Crenshaw pointed out that anti-discrimination law often underplays the impacts of intersectional discrimination by focusing only on one or other element at work in the complex.[15] "Intersectionality" is a concept since widely taken up in social analysis beyond legal theory, whether in academic scholarship, public discourse, or even in the media in the U.S. and globally. I discuss intersectionality in contrast with colorblindness in Chapter 6 below.

Narrative

CRT 1.0 supplements its standard methodologies of legal and social analysis with one of narrative. Narrative and storytelling are meant to illustrate and render vivid the everyday impacts, the lived experiences, of legal and regulative application, their felt effects. Narrative offers a way for the voices and accounts of the racially marginalized, often lost in data and abstract analytic tools, to provide insight and evidence, otherwise unavailable, of the challenges they face. As a supplement not a substitute for legal analysis and sociological data, narrative brings to life the debilitating outcomes of legally structured racial discrimination.

*

It should be obvious that little if any distinction is drawn by conservative critics between Critical Race Theory (CRT 1.0) and Critical Race Studies (CRS). Critical Race Studies is the broader, loosely affiliated smorgasbord of theories developed over the past four decades. The theories have been taken up, fiercely debated, and sometimes dismissed across the expansive analysis of race and racism in and beyond the academy. Notwithstanding the caricature by CRT's radical conservative critics, there are significant distinctions among the broad array of theories lumped together under the same conceptual roof.

Anthony Appiah is a prominent philosopher who is critical of race and racism. Following earlier analysts such as anthropologist Franz Boas and geneticist Richard Lewontin, Appiah has pointed out that the racial *differences* between members taken to belong to the same racial group are invariably greater than the differences between members of different racial groups. Appiah's insight may be applied to critical race work too: The contrasts between those who engage in "critical race studies" in the broad are often as great as between those who do and do not. And there are significant distinctions between those who practice Critical Race Theory in the legal conception

(CRT 1.0) and many of those engaged in Critical Race Studies (CRS) more broadly understood. To reduce them all to a singular view, especially to dismiss them all as invidious, is academically tantamount to saying that all members of this or that racial or ethnic group cannot be told apart. It is like proclaiming members of a given racial group are identical in look, thought, or behavior. And it is more or less as pernicious.

For CRT 1.0, then, law structures racial, gendered, and class inequalities interactively into the U.S. social system. These inequalities remain and are extended even when racial terms are not or ever were explicitly in use. The legal and administrative language may look or sound neutral; the effects are not. Similarly, CRS analyses reveal racial disparities in wealth and income, in property ownership, in employment, in tax policy, in school and college resources and access reproduced over time. Carol Anderson's historical work, for example, illustrates how absolutist commitments to Second Amendment gun rights have always been at the expense of Black life.[16] Her work shows, too, how the lines may blur between CRS and CRT 1.0 in far more compelling ways than radical critics like Rufo will admit.

This blurring can be found also in research on the stark racial and class disparities built into the lived environment. These disparities include access to clean water, accessible public transport, notably higher temperatures due to lack of green space in urban Black and Brown neighborhoods. But they also cover the lack of easily accessible, nutritional, and affordable food sources, and supermarkets in racially segregated, under-resourced neighborhoods. These differences are often directly traceable to the legacy of legal redlining from the mid-1930s to the late 1960s, as I demonstrate in more detail in Chapter 5. Hence the analytic entanglements of CRT 1.0 and CRS.

*

CRT 1.0 offers a jurisprudential and social theory. As such, it is open to critique and development, even rejection with due counterargument. Careful critical analysis and counterargument regarding CRT 1.0 or CRS have all been notably absent from the Trufer attacks. These attacks hurl charges, largely unbacked by citational reference and data, glossed in ways unrelated to what is quoted, or in some instances completely made up.

Here's one far from isolated example. Identifying Andrew Hacker as a "critical race theorist" (an identity Hacker nowhere expressed interest in assuming), Christopher Rufo dismisses him as asserting that "America is a fundamentally racist society."[17] Hacker's point, borne out by extensive data, is that the American social system by the early 1990s continued to limit Black people's opportunities for decent housing, schooling, employment, and health care in ways reaffirming the 1967 Kerner Report. Hacker comes down on the side of social structure as the driving force positioning people unequally. Individual agency can only be exercised within the confines of structural conditions.

The story CRT tells about America, then, is that it was structured from the outset to be controlled by and to advantage wealthier white men and those under their spheres of influence. Less wealthy whites generally benefitted by being positioned to help preserve the prevailing structure. In the process they accumulated privileges and possibilities not otherwise available to them. When their powers, advantages, and privileges were seemingly threatened, whites more readily bandied together to secure their historical and inherited benefits. Critical race theorists generally think America is facing just such a moment.

I turn, in Part II, to address the claims being made to these effects.

Part II

Fabrications

4

A Method of Misreading

What has Christopher Rufo "seen" regarding Critical Race Theory? There are many sites and sightings from which to draw. It is best, then, to hew closely to Rufo's own definitive CRT statements. Fortunately, he has summarized his basic representations in an eighteen-minute YouTube "video-essay" he produced and in which he serves as the authoritative voice.[1] The video composition has been viewed a quarter of a million times. It is, in turn, supplemented by published material. The most notable but far from only contribution is a go-to "Critical Race Theory Briefing Book"[2] Rufo has put together for the uninitiated and fellow activists. It combines in one place the litany of claims he made in the Heritage and Manhattan Institute articles mentioned earlier. The Heritage Foundation now has its own version of such a book. It is little different from Rufo's.

Rufo's video-essay is a quite effective piece of agitprop, superficially slick, quick in claim and pace. His talking head is intercut with found images and computational graphics. "CRT," Rufo declares at the outset, is "the new orthodoxy in America's public institutions." If "[m]ost Americans have no idea where [CRT] comes from or the society it envisions," it is left to Rufo to show us that it is around every corner, "why it is a threat to the country, and most importantly . . . how you can fight it."

Research, analytic carefulness, and fact-checking, nevertheless, are not the strong suits of Rufo and company, to put it generously. As we will see in the following chapters, they mostly misread quotes they provide in supposed evidence of their projections about CRT. They mischaracterize examples they offer to bear out their criticisms. They do so, more often than not, by leaving out key details and context, or reading into the examples an intentionality for which there is scant evidence. Trufers make a method of misreading.

Focusing exclusively on these misdirections, though important, may be to miss the key point, however. Rufo and the Trufers are singing to another tune, playing offkey from a different song book. Rufo seems to project an image of himself as guilelessly leading the church choir. He is actually fronting for the white power metal band.

Rufo and his followers care less about accuracy. Their point is make-believe. If tweets are something like the medium of the political unconscious today, Rufo himself reveals his complete lack of concern with accuracy. In fact, he is baldly explicit about this in a rare if unintended moment of Twitter self-revelation. In March 2021, RealChrisRufo⚔ tweeted about his defining strategy:

> We have successfully frozen their brand – 'critical race theory' – into the public conversation and are steadily driving up negative perceptions. We will eventually turn it toxic, as we put all of the various cultural insanities under that brand category.

He continues:

> The goal is to have the public read something crazy in the newspaper and immediately think 'critical race theory.' We

have decodified the term and will recodify it to annex the entire range of cultural constructions that are unpopular with Americans.[3]

RealChrisRufo✕ expanded on this strategy of political fabrication three months later:

> If you want to see public policy outcomes you have to run a public persuasion campaign.

Rufo's role, by his own admission, has been to characterize negatively for political ends those research programs in any way critical of race and racism.

> I basically took that body of criticism, I paired it with breaking news stories that were shocking and explicit and horrifying, and made it political . . . Turned it into a salient political issue with a clear villain.[4]

All of conservative America's driving demons are rolled into the singular villain of "CRT." One has to admire the efficiency and effectivity in the hubris. RealChrisRufo✕, arch white political savior, St. George slaying the Dragon.

Rufo has learned well the lessons from his crusading predecessors. The Southern Strategy has been taken to school.[5] He deployed the example of Campus Watch, David Horowitz's initiative designed to identify and publicly disparage any college activity it regarded as leftist. Rufo adapted this to apply first and foremost to K-12 schools and only as an afterthought to college campuses. Get 'em young. Turning Point USA is conservative activist Charlie Kirk's incendiary operation to promote radical right-wing values in schools and on college campuses. James O'Keefe is the far-right political activist whose Project Veritas has a history of running misleadingly venomous campaigns to entrap progressive politicians, activists, and scholars. Rufo has combined these strategies effectively, veiling the venom behind a façade of sweetness. The aim is to have any critic of racism look, through selective editing, like they are expressing themselves in self-implosive ways. Rufo, in short, is the second coming of Dinesh D'Souza, who for a couple of decades from the 1990s took aim first at academics and then at politicians like Barack Obama and Hillary Clinton with trumped-up characterizations.[6]

From Kirk and O'Keefe Rufo has taken the lesson to be outrageously bold and pay little consequence for perverse conspiracy claims. From Horowitz he has learned that, once made, false charges have an ongoing life almost impossible to erase. And from D'Souza, with whom he shares something of a documentary filmmaking background, he quickly saw the power of the make-believe narrative. The political reach of Trufism has much exceeded all of his predecessors' efforts, perhaps in good part because of his façade of earnest innocence. It has been aided no doubt by Presidential trumpeting and tapping into the morphing of illiberal anger from disagreement to insurrection, alienation to violence. Rufo, to put it pithily, has deeply absorbed the lesson plan for the self-appointed moral police.

As the nominal voice, Rufo has been aided by a seeming mildness of personal character, a soft assertiveness of falsity, a self-assurance when on friendly ground. Challenged by less convinced interviewers for more even-handed and critical publications and media forums, as he sometimes has been, Rufo often turns from an appearance of guilelessness to being less unflappable, more evasive, sometimes seemingly churlish. The critical storm can sting. Especially when one's house has been built on quicksand.

Fabrication runs all the way through, the very method in the making of the mania. It can be discerned at the outset as the shared mark of both Rufo's video and Briefing Book. Simple fact-checking shows that virtually every claim about "CRT" (which is why I sometimes put the term in quote marks, since the Trufers are attacking a phantom) is outright false, twisted to portray its least agreeable interpretation, or at best half-true – which is, by implication, also to say half-lie. White lies of another dimension. Designer templates for gaslighting.

Rufo's public façade of earnest sincerity is belied by the materials he has produced taking aim at CRT. He and his Trufer followers frame CRT in completely misleading historical, intellectual, and political terms. The Briefing Book makes Rufo's rhetorical strategy repeatedly clear. CRT is taken by him and his supporters to include not just the more widely scattered field of CRS but also less obviously *any* criticism of racism. For all dismissive points, they offer just one example or at most a very limited number to bear out the extreme assertion, where the least favorable interpretation is attributed to the short, decontextualized passage cited. And then this is generalized to all of CRT and CRS, to all critical accounts of race and racism.[7]

Like CRT 1.0, the Rufoist doctrine is committed to a small set of key characterizations regarding "CRT." They tell a very different story from the account by CRT 1.0's original architects as summarized in Chapter 3 above. Over the next chapters, let's assess these CRT fabrications in turn, from the rejection of any contemporary structural racism (Chapter 5) to the embrace of colorblindness (Chapter 6), and the completely make-believe history of CRT (Chapter 7).

5

~~Structural Racism~~?

Enduring structural and systemic racism in the U.S. is one formulation foundational to CRT, uniting 1.0 and CRS: for CRT and CRS, racism is endemic to American life. Trufers extrapolate from this that CRT aims to bury the present in America's past history, denying progress. Racism for "Critical Race Theory," they conclude, is an irrepressible and endless feature of American life, overriding all else. So, the question is whether structural racism no longer (significantly) marks American society, as Rufo and his band think.

Florida Republican Congressman Byron Donalds, taking his cue from Rufo, asserts that CRT sets out to "trap" Americans by "the scars of our nation."[1] Donalds, one of only two Black Republican U.S. Representatives, expresses an idea central to current conservative thinking concerning racism. Rufoist-style critics emphatically confine structural or systemic racism in the U.S. to the distant past. While defending his declaration of April as "Confederate History Month" to "honor the lost lives in the war," Mississippi Governor Tate Reeves denied "systemic racism in America." The leading Republican candidate for California Governor in the 2020 Republican-fueled recall election was libertarian radio host, Larry Elder. He declared on the campaign trail, again without argument, that "Systemic racism is not the problem and critical race theory and reparations are not the answer."[2] I suppose political campaigning requires bald contentions without reasons. Earlier in 2021 Elder wrote that "Obama's own presidential victory demonstrates that America is not systemically racist." Florida Congresswoman Ileana Garcia makes the same point. Elder added that he "know(s) there is no evidence of anti-Black 'systemic racism' on the part of the police,"[3] without offering any source for his revelation.

Elder's implication, like Rufo's, is that any contemporary racism is negligible, and strictly individual, the product of a bad apple here or there. While never clearly stated, the suggestion seems to be that structural racism was undone by the Civil Rights Act of 1964, borne out, if Elder is any indication, by Obama's eventual Presidential election. Racism supposedly prevents no one from getting ahead, by hard work, sacrifice, and ingenuity. Which, of course, implies that those not getting ahead are failing of their own accord. Radical anti-progressive Trufer opposition is to any critical race analysis they think holds that the U.S. is constitutively racist, that skin color is used to create and maintain social, economic, and political inequalities between whites and racial others.

Critical Race Theory is a philosophy, Rufo contends, relegating all white people to the role of oppressors and Black people to that of victims. A very small set of contributors to the larger, sprawling field of CRS may have expressed themselves in something like this way. The dominant version of Afropessimism, which is never targeted by Trufer critics and is increasingly criticized by CRT, can perhaps be read in this way. But it is far from a standard position. Overreach is the method of the underthought.

The foundational presumption of Trufism is that there is no more structural or systemic racism. This is a widely shared projection also in countries like France and Britain. In both the U.S. and Europe the claim that there are no longer active laws discriminating explicitly against people racially defined is taken as a sign of social progress and standing. Structural or systemic racism supposedly ended for the U.S. with the wave of the legislative wand in 1964. In France and Britain, conservatives seem to doubt it ever existed. The French state, for example, ignores the fact that Muslims in its prisons make up at least four times their proportion of the general population. In the Netherlands, citizens of color with family backgrounds from the former colonies of Suriname and the Antilles face rates of unemployment two to three times higher than whites. Across mainland Europe, the post-World War II restriction on collecting racial or ethnically indexed social data, including with census-taking, makes it extremely difficult to identify discriminatory social trends. Far from discouraging structural discrimination in these societies, such restrictions become a feature of it.

Trufists appear to advance just a single argument for their denial of contemporary structural racism. Equality of opportunity not equitable outcome or impact, they declare, should solely underpin a just society. Everyone, the presumption goes, should equally have opportunities to advance their life conditions through effort, hard, work, and smarts. It does not follow from this, note, that Trufists are committed to the opportunities being the same. Where people end up requires nothing more from the state than guaranteeing they face no formal external barriers in their opportunities to succeed. Those who fail, the implication has it, would have none of the qualities to thrive, and bear the only responsibility.

If structural racism ever characterized the U.S., on this dismissive view, it was because equality of opportunity was historically undercut by racial discrimination written into legislation (segregated education or neighborhoods, discriminatory hiring, and voting discouragement protected by law). As none of this explicitly exists anymore, the neo-conservative argument concludes, the problems of systemic and structural racism have been erased.

This Trufer account is far too quick and facile. Consider the national practice of redlining, which existed as formal Federal Housing Authority (FHA) policy from the late 1930s to the end of the 1960s. FHA regulations simply formalized what had been widely practiced well before, and has continued since. Racial covenants were contracts usually issued by homeowner associations legally restricting white homeowners from selling their property especially to Black people in "white neighborhoods." They were finally ruled illegal only in 1968, in a parallel ruling to end redlining. The effects of both, however, were never reversed.

Redlining structured residential segregation into urban landscapes across America. The National Archives house FHA maps indicating redlined areas for 239 cities across America.[4] Redlining was designed and reinforced explicitly through the law, municipal rules, and mortgage policy. Blacks and those of Mexican descent were explicitly confined to purchasing residential property in redlined areas, facing greater hurdles and higher rates in securing mortgages because they were marked as credit risks. Whites could purchase in zones designated on maps in blue and green. These zones had more greenery and space as well as resources invested in them, in ways reproduced ever since. The widespread practice of redlining underpinned the development of segregated white suburbia, leaving behind resource-challenged inner-city neighborhoods and segregated towns.

Take two people, one Black, one white, of equal wealth. Each sought to purchase real estate in the late 1930s after the FHA institutionalized redlining. Assume the Black man purchased a property in a redlined area, at a price, say, of $30,000. The white person purchased property in a blue or green zone, say, at $100,000. Fast forward to the present, with the properties inherited by their respective families. Assume, modestly, in each case price acceleration of 15 (price acceleration in the redlined area was likely to be considerably less than in blue and green defined spaces). The current values of those properties would be $450,000 versus $1.5 million respectively. So, the differentials in contemporary wealth have been structured historically into our social arrangements, through no personal doing.

Rufo and his crowd are deeply skeptical of hypotheticals, so consider an actual case. In 1912, Willa and Charles Bruce purchased a beachfront property in Manhattan Beach, California for approximately $1,250 (hard to believe in our time). They established a seaside resort catering for Black families when Los Angeles beaches were openly hostile to the presence of Black beachgoers. In 1924, concerned with Black presence in the city, the municipality exercised eminent domain, taking over the property ostensibly for a public park. The city paid the Bruces $14,000 (today approximately $225,000), significantly less than its then market value. The Bruces were subjected to an onslaught of local racist abuse, and they moved out of the town. No park was ever established.

In recent years, the Bruce family sought return or restitution. The city had transferred the property to Los Angeles County with the agreement it could not be privately owned, making return complicated if not impossible. The land is estimated to be worth at least $75 million (an acceleration rate of well over 300). The city, with its Black population just one percent (California's Black population is 6.5 percent), resisted both repatriation of the land and an apology to the Bruce family. (The city subsequently agreed to an acknowledgment and condemnation of the historical treatment, refusing apology on grounds of legal liability and that current residents bear no responsibility for the historical acts.) In 2021, an agreement was reached between county and family, the state legislature, and Governor Gavin Newsom to remove ordinances standing in the way of the return. In September 2021, the property was returned to the family, Newsom apologizing to them in person on behalf of the state.[5]

In short, the Bruce family enjoyed some measure of restitution, even though they had been forced to move, dispossessed of wealth that would have placed them in much better stead than they suffered as a result, and subjected to extended racism. The outcome, largely driven and brokered by local Manhattan Beach resident activist Kavon Ward, signals at least one way, among others, to provide a semblance of reparative justice.[6] Ms. Ward has started a movement, "Reclaim My Land," to help Black families nationally repossess property historically stripped from them.

This example, far from isolated, offers an instance of how structures of enduring racism with significant material impact are built into the system. In Minneapolis, just 25 percent of Black residents own their homes, while more than 75 percent of whites do, a function of the historic segregation, dispossession, and disinheritance effected by redlining. Nationally, Black family home ownership stands at 42 percent, 30 percent less than white families (the racial gap is higher by three points than it was in 1960). Residential segregation, copious data has shown, underpins educational, employment, and, as a result, opportunity segregation. Those living in areas that were formally redlined, in cities large and small, are overwhelmingly Latino and Black. They continue, at all socio-economic levels, to face significantly higher rates of disease-causing pollution as a result of closer proximity to coal-burning plants, polluting industry, and highways. Data show that whites disproportionately generate air pollution, while Blacks and Latinos overwhelmingly bear the costs.[7] Redlining, in short, has anchored lifetimes of structured inequality cross-generationally.

Nathan Nunn and his Economic History students at Harvard University have tracked the impacts to which the Tulsa Massacre and razing of the segregated Black neighborhood of Greenwood in 1921 directly led. Following the massacre (up to

300 Black people were killed), there was a 45 percent decline in Black home ownership in Tulsa, in employment by Blacks in white-collar occupations like lawyers, doctors, and journalists, and a 33 percent average decline in earnings. But there were indirect "spillover" effects as well, in segregated parts of the country. Their research shows a 12 to 15 percent national decline in Black home ownership and wealth. Violent events against Black communities throughout the twentieth century, they argue, likely explain the enduring inequalities between Black and white wealth, what Du Bois famously called "wages of whiteness."[8]

Repeated tests and studies continue to demonstrate that, nationally, appraisals of the same home when thought by white appraisers to be white-owned come in as much as 40 percent higher in value than when thought to be Black-owned. More than 90 percent of home appraisers in the U.S. are white. These variances in value in turn impact the capacity to secure a mortgage, the rate of interest, sales price for the home, and so wealth.[9] While less well documented, there is considerable evidence of discrimination in rental and home-buying markets throughout much of Europe too.[10]

In his arch-conservative bestseller, *American Marxism*,[11] Mark Levin writes approvingly that there is "massive economic redistribution" along racial lines in America. If so, how is it that the median wealth of Black Americans, as determined by the Federal Reserve in 2019 at a little over $24,000, remains a fragment of white American wealth, a touch over $188,000? For Latinos it is $36,000.[12] Or that in a wealthy city like Boston white median wealth is $247,000 while for Black Bostonians it is – wait for it – all of $8 (your eyes are not deceiving you, that is a single digit)? In August 2021, as the Covid Delta variant was surging and dampening hiring, especially across public-facing service industries, white unemployment dropped from 5.4 percent to 5.2 percent. Black unemployment increased from 8.2 to 8.8 percent. Prior to the pandemic, Black Americans were more likely to suffer food insecurity at 2.8 times the rate of whites. Over two years into the pandemic, that rate is 3.2 times, a function of unemployment, lower levels of savings, and lack of affordable food outlets. Since 2010, for all of Levin's "massive economic redistribution," inequality spiraled between wealthier whiter segments of the population and poorer, more racially diverse segments. On a presumption of nothing but individual responsibility, the relative praise and blame are purely a function of a person's effort and smarts. Racial genes seem to lurk surreptitiously in the shadows of Levin's rhetoric.

The effects of systemic racism are etched structurally into the system in all sorts of less visible ways. And they follow people to their graves, literally. In Oberlin, Louisiana, a Black policeman was denied burial in a local cemetery in a town he had served for fifteen years. The burial contract mandated the burial ground "was for the remains of white human beings only," effectively a racial covenant for cemeteries. The year of the burial covenant was not 1921, or 1951. It was 2021. When the burial ground apologetically sought to annul the old racist contracts, a white man sued. The ACLU attempts to desegregate the cemetery, he charged, violated his contract to be buried in an all-white cemetery. "I am not racist," he proclaimed, but "prefers" being buried with "his kind."[13]

Rufo's chorus is that CRT is "anti-capitalist." He charges that it advocates for "anti-capitalist forced redistribution of property." Both within CRT 1.0 and across the wider span of CRS, a broad spectrum of views about capitalism and property pertains, far from reducible to Rufo's reductive characterization. To take his own favorite "CRT" demons, Ibram X. Kendi indeed identifies racism with capitalism, and calls for the latter's abolition as an abiding anti-racist commitment. But, as Charles Mills's work has exemplified, one need not be a Marxist to identify racism with capitalism.[14] Or, to take another, Robin DiAngelo nowhere commits to this position, and the tenor of her argument makes her much more comfortable with classical philosophical liberalism. She appears quite at ease with wealth and private property. All three have declared they are not critical race theorists. Rufo readily tries to turn CRT tied to CRS into a monolith in order to demonize all of it at once. But he can do so only by dramatically distorting the range of views at issue.

One demonstration of such distortion, among the wide array at play, is Rufo's repeated invocation of a classic CRT 1.0 article, Cheryl Harris's "Whiteness as Property" (in the Briefing Book one of only two short CRT 1.0 references he invokes).[15] Rufo and his followers take Harris's 100-page law publication to say that property in the U.S. is constitutionally white. That's a provocative idea, but it is not one Harris advances. Whiteness for her is a *status* property, "the settled *expectations* that are to be protected" in law (my emphasis). The structure of law has enabled and protected historically established property rights for whites. In this, whiteness has value, operates *as if* property. This is the very converse of Rufo's charge that for Harris property is white. Racial covenants established or extended segregated residential areas artificially elevating property values well after such covenants were rendered unconstitutional. The Manhattan Beach example bears this out, offering one of many cases in which race, class, and law reinforce each other.

Characterizing "Whiteness as Property" to be reductively about physical property, then, is a bit like referring to Robert Musil's classic 1930 novel, *The Man Without Qualities*, as being about "a man without property." Both would-be interpretations commit a category mistake, the result of an acute misreading. The question is not whether Cheryl Harris is Marxist; it is what is in her text. Harris does not propose "suspending private property rights," "seizing land and wealth from the rich" or "redistributing [private property] along racial lines," as Rufoists repeatedly charge. She actually closes the probing article with a rather modest proposal for affirmative action, not a "revolutionary" one of property revocation and "forced redistribution."

Affirmative action, it should be emphasized, has in the past been found constitutional by repeated if careful Supreme Court majorities, from Lewis Powell's majority decision in *Bakke vs. University of California*, in 1978, to Anthony Kennedy's majority opinion in *Fisher vs. University of Texas*, in 2016.[16] Neither Justice can believably be labeled a "radical" or "revolutionary." Or, for all of it, a critical race theorist. Similarly, the European Union continues to support policies of "positive discrimination" in pursuit "of a more egalitarian society." Nothing Rufo has said on record acknowledges any of this.

*

In summary, then, Trufers' fabricating strategy operates on three interlacing trajectories. It seeks to preserve advantages for whites built into the social foundations. It de-means terms such as "racism" of their critical charge. The "demeaning" is effected both by flippantly de-emphasizing the force of racisms' legacy and devaluing the conventional critical terms used to characterize that legacy.[17] Vladimir Putin's "de-nazification of Ukraine" as his rationalization of Russian invasion perfectly exemplifies this modality. And third, this advantage preservation through demeaning (in both senses) is shored up by the *deregulating of racism*, its renewed licensing, in ways I will elaborate in Part III. A few more critical moves are still needed to clear the way forward, however.

6

The Gospel of Colorblindness

Intersectionality, we saw in Chapter 3, is a concept popularized by CRT 1.0. It is designed to capture not just overlapping but the ramifying modes of discrimination people can suffer as a result of membership of multiple groups uniquely targeted for inequitable or partial treatment. In thinking structural racism a thing of the past, Rufo and his followers are dismissive of such claims, deeming them overblown.

Trufers generally misconceive the notion of intersectionality. Levin, for example, thinks of it more like parallelism, a claim about multiple kinds and sources of parallel discrimination running alongside each other.

> [O]ften individuals and groups are said to be victims of more than one kind of discrimination. For example, if an individual is female, Muslim, and Black, she is said to be subjected to multiple forms of discrimination. This, too, has been given a name by, among others, University of California, Los Angeles, law professor Kimberlé Crenshaw – intersectionality.[1]

Levin's gloss embeds the understanding common to CRT's Trufist critics that for critical race theorists race eclipses any other discrimination. CRTers will have one judged, as Rufo and company repeatedly emphasize, only by one's race.[2] "But human beings," Levin adds a page on, "are more than racial beings," insinuating that for CRT they are not.

"Intersectionality" in Crenshaw's hands, however, operates more subtly than Levin projects. The point is not simply that there are multiple forms of parallel discrimination. It signals, rather, a more complex social state: where a person or group is subjected to multiple modes of discrimination they tend to reinforce and multiply their interacting impacts at their point(s) of intersection. These discriminatory intersections produce unique, and uniquely intensified, social debilitations in the specific circumstances of those experiencing them.

When Amy Cooper called police to complain about an "African-American man threatening" to harm her on a bright day in Manhattan's Central Park she was self-evidently doing so *because* he was a man *and* Black. It may be a more open question had the person asking been a Black woman. Open to question is how likely Ms. Cooper would have been to call 911 had the person been a white man or white woman. At the very least, she would likely not have exclaimed to the police that a "*white* man (or woman)" was threatening her. All Christian Cooper (no relation to Amy) was asking her to do was to obey park rules by leashing her dog. Had she obliged instead of hand-restraining the dog while dialing, nothing more would have come of it. She conceded as much in a social media apology posted the day following the incident.

Apology notwithstanding, Amy Cooper subsequently filed a civil suit against her former employer for wrongful termination resulting from the incident's fallout. In the suit, which the court rejected, she charged Christian with "a history" of "aggressively confronting dog owners in Central Park without a leash . . . caus[ing] dog owners to be fearful for their safety and the safety of their dogs." Of course, she could not have known of this "history" at the time of her call, and no one else had previously reported him. Her call smacks of "a history" rather of characterizing Black men as "aggressive" and "threatening." It is the work of critical race analysis to work out these modes of intersecting reinforcement and ramification, their conditions of prompting and their systemic and contextual effects. Christian, to his credit, thinks Amy has suffered enough, and ought now to be left alone.

I have seen no serious CRT 1.0 scholar committed to the Trufist projection that, in intersection "with other victimization categories" like gender, "race is *always* primary" (my emphasis). The point of intersectional analysis properly applied is that conditions and context dictate what the primary and exacerbating determinants of inequality and victimization are in specific circumstances. Intersectionality's insight is that analysts have to examine the circumstances to tease out what if any category may be most determining. A Black Vietnam vet confined to a wheelchair may have been denied access to a swank night club for different if partly overlapping reasons than, say, the likes of Vito Russo in "Midnight Cowboy" or Luke Martin in "Coming Home." "Superman" Christopher Reeves likely would not have been denied at all.

*

"Colorblindness" remains the go-to default for conservative talking points on race. Trufers are quick to invoke Martin Luther King's famous words not to be judged "by the color of [one's] skin but the content of [one's] character." Few of Rufo's crowd have bothered to register the source of King's remarks, or what preceded the phrase in his 1963 speech. And they rarely quote the remarks accurately. King's rhetorical reach for being judged on character was explicitly aspirational: "I have a dream," he reiterated throughout the address across the Washington Mall. Trufers hear only the waving of the magic wand to erase history and leave material conditions untouched so that guiltless colorblindness becomes the social default. By contrast, King's aspiration that his "four little children will one day live in a nation where they will not be judged" by race could be realized, as the speech repeatedly emphasizes, only once the conditions and impacts of structural racism have been successfully addressed. All of King's work between the passing of the Civil Rights Act in 1964 and his assassination in 1968 makes clear that, were he alive, he would hardly be saying that structural racism has ceased to define life in America, Europe, or its (former) colonies. Quite the contrary.

It is ironic that MLK should be so readily invoked by the Trufers. They are all too quick to drown CRT in charges of "Marxism" and "communism." They nevertheless appear utterly oblivious to the fact that King was branded in the 1960s by FBI Director J. Edgar Hoover and his circle in exactly these terms. Trufers, it seems, have come almost full circle.

The European analogue to the American embrace of color-blindness has been the post-World War II rush to require a state standard of "non-racialism."[3] Rhetorically, this generic adoption of racelessness blindfolds its proponents to the facts of structural racism described in small part above. EU member states cannot invoke "race" to characterize human difference at all, and racial categories are precluded from official census-taking or polling. In Germany, not uncommonly in EU states, people are classified as "German," "foreigner," or "German with a migration background." A million people of African background now live in Germany, a quarter with no migration background. These German categories thus are incapable of properly identifying the racial makeup of its population, and the conditions faced. In 2020, two Berlin-based civil society groups conducted a survey, "Afrozensus," of Afro-Germans. It found significant discrimination against Black Germans across every social register: housing, education, work, policing and the justice system, media (including the internet), and from public agencies. The pandemic exacerbated conditions, more than 12 percent reporting job loss as a result, far higher than the national average.[4]

As critics have repeatedly pointed out, colorblindness and racelessness – the individualizing response to structural and systemic racial injustice par excellence – hide the underlying structural differences historic inequalities reproduce. Those who claim to be colorblind or practice racelessness, "not to see race," are in fact revealing that they refuse to "see" racially driven injustices at all.[5] That Trufers have not identified anything else King was dreaming of in his extended address makes their myopia abundantly evident concerning the material structures of racism, and their effects.

Justice John Marshall Harlan was the first major figure to make a public legal pitch for colorblindness. *Plessy v. Ferguson* (1896) was the Supreme Court case famously granting states constitutional protection to segregate public facilities like railway coaches, drinking fountains, and theaters. Harlan was the lone dissenter. He definitively pointed out in his dissenting opinion that "the white race" has nothing to fear from

> "colorblindness" given its "dominan[ce] . . . in prestige, in achievements, in education, in wealth and in power. . . . it will continue to be for all time, if it remains true to its great heritage and holds fast to the principles of constitutional liberty."[6]

Harlan was an interesting flag-bearer for the cause. He had grown up in a slave-holding household, which included a mixed-race, enslaved half-brother, Robert. (There is some question as to whether Robert was the son of John Harlan's father, James, or of John's grandfather, or whether Robert was purchased as a young boy by James and informally adopted.) Robert purchased his own freedom from the family and acquired considerable wealth across the rest of his life (he would eventually befriend Ulysses Grant, play a role in the Republican Party, and get elected, during Reconstruction, to the Ohio House of Representatives). John Marshall Harlan inherited twelve slaves from his late father, whom he eventually freed when required by the Thirteenth Amendment three decades before *Plessy*. He had actually opposed the Reconstruction Amendments abolishing slavery and establishing formal equality and the right to vote. But, over the next decade, he grew to become an advocate for them. Harlan's story exemplifies the entangled social history of race that clearly remains alive, even when buried beneath colorblindness.

What Harlan emphasized in a rare moment of racial honesty is that "the principles of constitutional liberty" will continue to reproduce and multiply the racially ordered inequalities advantaging whites constructed at the historical outset into the social structures defining the country.

Take one revealing example. In 2013, the Supreme Court struck down what had been a key Voting Rights Act requirement since 1965 (*Shelby County v. Holder*). Certain states would no longer have to receive "pre-clearance" from the U.S. Justice Department for voting system changes in those states in order to ensure Black voters would not, again, be more readily disparately impacted by the proposed changes than white voters, as they had been especially prior to 1965. Writing for the majority, Justice Samuel Alito opined that "some disparity in impact does not mean a system [here, of voting] is not equally open."[7] So a system the impact of which, no matter lawmakers' stated intentions, repeatedly makes it somewhat more difficult for Blacks than whites to vote, and by implication dampens Black voter turnout election after election, would not suffice to register the Court's concerns over racial disparity. The law, after all, is meant to be – and on Alito's consideration *is* – colorblind.

Many critics of this ruling would recognize Alito's finding to be a way of legally structuring racial disbenefits to Blacks into a key social system. An important question to ask, one Trufers would prefer to close down, is whether racial impact consistently disadvantaging Blacks for the benefits of whites – Blacks face barriers meant to discourage voting so whites more readily get to maintain political power – is not a classic form of structural racism.

*

The formalized mechanisms of segregation, Harlan and Heritage concur,[8] are not needed anymore to maintain white privilege and political power. The Trufist stress on untethered individual freedom parading as colorblindness, whether to say or do whatever one will, is all that is needed to reproduce the racial advantage. Just as she did in the late 1980s for "everyday racism," Philomena Essed has coined the concept for this condition. She has called it "entitlement racism." Entitlement racism self-authorizes to do or say anything racially charged, to deny the racial significance, and to benefit from the advantage or suffer little if any consequence as a result.[9]

Colorblindness with no content, racelessness without legal bite, then, has become the anti-CRT anthem, Trufism's default chorus-line. Rufo's reach for colorblindness, as I have stressed, is the insistence on individual agency, while ignoring that structural conditions shape possibility. This Gospel of Colorblindness, an article of unquestioned faith, effectively renders segregation the outcome of seemingly neutral informal determinants like individual preferences and market forces. In informalizing segregation, colorblindness and racelessness more generally render it pretty much legally untouchable. They effectively deregulate segregation, removing it from government oversight, regulation, and curtailment.

Crenshaw's intersectionality, by contrast, implies the recognition that structural racism elevates some, while debilitating possibilities for others. Colorblinding commitments tend to cover up historically inherited structural disadvantages faced by members of particular groups, curtailing life's possibilities. At the same time, they liberate disparaging "race-free" characterizations of those suffering these curtailments. "Intersectionality" is a term of analytic art formulated to make evident discriminations otherwise more hidden from view, not least by the activation of colorblindness and modes of racelessness in everyday life. Colorblinding and racelessness work to cover up racisms. Intersectionality serves to surface them.

7

Fictive Histories

In seeking to dismiss CRT, Rufo includes a back story, taking himself to be laying out the definitive historical emergence and formation of CRT, its driving influences and (hidden) agenda. Foundational to his back story is that "CRT" sought to update Marxism. It supposedly inherited its structure of thinking from the "neo-Marxists" of Critical Theory, "Walter Benjamin, Theodor Adorno, Max Horkheimer, and Harold Marcuse," CRT's purported forerunners. Realizing "in the 1960s" the actual failures of Marxist "brutality," Rufo maintains that "critical theorists abandoned the old economic dialectic of bourgeois and proletariat and replaced it with a new racial dialectic of white and Black."[1]

Is this narrative plausible? It is hard to gauge where exactly Rufo is finding this in the original CRT literature, whether in CRT 1.0 or in Critical Race Studies (CRS). Some in the more sprawling field of CRS – far from all – may have been influenced by one or other of the figures named here. Yet there is no evidence, as I demonstrate below, and Rufo and his followers offer no textual demonstration, that any CRT thinkers hold that they substituted race for class in the way projected. Nothing warrants the sort of substitution Rufo and those he has inspired suggest.

There are four related embarrassments to this Trufist vision. First, the only driving influences on CRT Trufers seem to recognize are white German Jewish men. No Black, Brown, Asian or women intellectual forerunners, American or globally, nor any non-Jewish whites. It sounds a bit like the Rothschild banking conspiracy, or Soros's control of the deep state. CRT 1.0 or CRS are obviously taken to have no sources of influence who are not white men! No Frederick Douglass, W.E.B. Du Bois, Zora Neale Hurston, Fannie Lou Hamer, Frantz Fanon, Aimé Césaire, Alain Locke, Hannah Arendt, Charles Hamilton Houston, Stokely Carmichael and Charles Hamilton, Derrick Bell, Audre Lorde, on and on.

The list of CRT's supposed father-figures seems to support the complaint that CRT is "neo-Marxist."[2] This misunderstands the landscape of academic theorizing. Marxist analyses are one among many inhabitants of this landscape, offering diverse ways of understanding social arrangements. To take its contributions seriously is consistent with taking liberal and conservative analysis seriously. Rousseau, Hume, Kant, Wollstonecraft, Marx, Mill, Weber, Von Hayek, Schmitt, and Keynes have the same standing for any serious analytic eye. They are those, among others, from whom the European philosophical and political traditions have derived ideas about equality and liberty, sources of exploitation, alienation, and injustice, authority and sovereignty, bureaucracy and the state. To those ideas we have come to add, in the past half-century, concerns about the fundamental impacts of gender and race in society, and so the contributions of those such as Hannah Arendt, W.E.B. Du Bois, Frantz Fanon, Edward Said, Audre Lorde, Gloria Anzaldúa, Angela Davis, Judith Butler, and Stuart Hall. The point here is not CRT's disparaged influences but the quality of its arguments and insights, which Trufers never actually discuss. CRT, as standard racist practice would have it, is taken by Rufo and company to have no mind of its own.

Second, Walter Benjamin was one of the German quartet not around in the 1960s. He did not survive the Nazi onslaught. On the most reliable accounts, he committed suicide in 1940 at the French-Spanish border attempting to flee murderous anti-Semitism nipping at his heels. It is a tragic story. The small group with which he was traveling was denied entry into Spain. He was fearful the Nazis would soon catch up with them, and so he drank the proverbial hemlock that night. The group received safe passage into Spain the next day. Adorno and Horkheimer, having spent a decade in the U.S., mostly in Los Angeles, taking refuge from the war, returned to Frankfurt to re-establish the Institute for Social Research, in 1949. They were hardly the revolutionary race thinkers Trufers are making them out to be.

Third, Adorno, Horkheimer, and Benjamin confined pretty much any discussion they devoted to racism exclusively to anti-Semitism and European fascism. This is perhaps understandable given their own experiences. Other than a much-criticized account taking issue with jazz and atonal music, Adorno, like Horkheimer, wrote nothing substantial about Black–white struggles, in the U.S. or anywhere else. Marcuse, who spent a much larger part of his adult life in the U.S.,[3] did make passing reference to racial struggles, but only briefly, to exemplify larger principles of his social analysis. To suggest that Marcuse offers a theory of racism when referring to "minority persecution" as the grounds for "uprising" is like saying that a video-game theorist who cites "World of Warcraft" as embedding lessons on moral reasoning is offering a theory of war.[4]

It is true that Angela Davis was a student both at the Frankfurt School and with Marcuse in the U.S. But, when she and others pressed Adorno to attend to "the standpoint of the oppressed," his dismissive response was to stress his commitment to bringing about "the dissolution of standpoint thinking itself." This hardly jibes with someone supposedly driven to replace one set of standpoints with another. Judge me not by the color of my thinking but the content of its character!

Rufo would appear to find historical research challenging. All it would require to check the details laid out in these first three points, short of reading up on the widely available historical accounts of the Frankfurt School, would be to have checked that hardly obscure encyclopedia, Wikipedia. Rufo's failure to do so can only be interpreted as the refusal to consider anything that would call his fabrications into question.

As if these details were not pulling the plug on the Trufer microphone finally, a bit more obscure fact-checking shows just how far the fabrications run. The prime reader for CRT 1.0, originally published in 1995, is edited by four among its principal founders, including Kimberlé Crenshaw.[5] The reader collects all the seminal articles, originally published in law journals, representing the onset of CRT 1.0. A nearly 500-page volume, it is repeatedly placed on display by Rufo as backdrop evidence in his video about CRT but also in video-recorded interviews he has given to the likes of the *New Yorker*. He seems to want to convey faux visual evidence of his "erudition," that he knows of which he speaks.

There are almost 1,500 footnotes included in the CRT 1.0 Reader (law articles are notoriously well-documented). Alas, had he checked, Rufo would have found not one single reference to Adorno, Horkheimer, Benjamin, or Marcuse. There are more references to Black conservative economist and political commentator Thomas Sowell and former U.S. Vice-President Hubert Humphrey (one each) than to Karl Marx. Outrageously, the references in the volume are overwhelmingly to U.S. legal cases, followed by the considerable tradition of Black American thinkers.

Rufo and some of those he has influenced also make repeated reference to the work of legal scholar Richard Delgado. References are almost exclusively to the little introductory survey of CRT 1.0 Delgado co-composed with fellow legal scholar Jean Stefancic in 2001. Having someone else do the hard work of synthesizing a large corpus of material beats having to make the effort oneself. Never referenced, however, is that, in 1995 too, Delgado likewise published a massive edited volume on CRT 1.0.[6] Nearly 600 pages and 50 articles in size, it rivals the other volume with 1,350 or so footnotes. There are a whopping two references to Marx, not as an embrace so much as passing reference, in a critical discussion of feminist Catherine MacKinnon's work by Angela Harris. And there is one additional reference, by indigenous legal scholar Roger Williams, to Walter Benjamin's biting remark about civilization always involving barbarism. There are more references in Delgado's collection to conservative commentator Shelby Steele (a roughly ten-page discussion) and to notorious nineteenth-century Justice John Marshall than to Marcuse, Horkheimer, and Adorno combined (the grand total of . . . zero).

The obvious rejoinder will be that the "neo-Marxist" influence is implicit, recognized by the initiated. This would entail the unproveable parading as the given. "Critical," however, etymologically means the capacity to judge the truth or merit of the object of analysis. This is the sense central to Immanuel Kant's foundational work in the late eighteenth century that set off the critical philosophical tradition. Trufist-inspired CRT criticisms exhibit none of these qualities. (To forestall further make-believe, Kant was the key founding philosopher of the Enlightenment, not straightforwardly of "critical theory," and, given his own views on race, he certainly offered no prototype for CRT. Far from "rejecting . . . the principles of the Enlightenment and the Age of Reason," as some have claimed, Kant nevertheless was the intellectual source for them, as anyone paying attention during their Philosophy 101 course would recognize.)[7]

Following Rufo, others expansively add that CRT simply substitutes "race struggle" for "class struggle" in the work of seminal left thinkers, like those previously mentioned, as well as Foucault, among others.[8] Michel Foucault generally gets a bad rap from Rufoists. He is notoriously difficult to pigeonhole. Conservatives generally identify him as a "leftist" though he distanced himself from Marxism increasingly after 1968. Of late, he has also been disparaged by some left critics, somewhat misleadingly I think, as having increasingly leaned "neoliberal" in later life because of his unqualified commitment to individual freedom and a deep skepticism of the modern state's disposition to constrain liberty. (In later lectures on neoliberalism, Foucault expressed passing appreciation of the doctrine's stress on freedom, not the same thing as adoption of neoliberal views.)[9] Foucault has indeed influenced some, again, far from all, who have contributed to CRS scholarship, but his idiosyncratic views on race and racism were largely translated into English only in the later 1990s, and had almost no impact on the earlier development of CRT 1.0.

Guy Sorman is a French economist living in the U.S. and a fellow traveler with Rufo at the Manhattan Institute, serving also on the editorial board of *City Journal*. In mid-2021 he "revealed" very publicly to have personally witnessed Foucault in April 1969 "raping" eight-year-old boys over gravestones in a Tunisian village cemetery. The problem with the accusation is that Foucault had returned in Fall 1968 to Paris following two years of teaching in Tunisia. The charges were quickly debunked by German journalists who traveled to Tunisia and interviewed village residents, who derided the claims.[10] It seems no make-believe is off-limits in these attacks on "CRT." Sorman later conceded the "error."

Those weighing in, including Rufo himself, appear neither to have read (properly or at all) the influences they suppose to have been exercised on CRT and mostly not any actual critical race theorists (in either the 1.0 or CRS versions). An example is thrown in, usually from Ibram X. Kendi, Robin DiAngelo and the like, a lifted quote here or there. The broader range of critics appear to have looked at little else than Rufo's articles and videos, from which almost all references are borrowed. Rufo's own references are less than a handful and invariably decontextualized.

It should be clear, then, that Rufo could care less what CRT in fact stands for. The terms "critical," "race," and "theory," he has repeatedly emphasized in public, are each super-charged fuel for the political right. Anything "critical" reads to them like a left-wing conspiracy. "Race" has become code both for what are deemed doomsday demographic shifts and, relatedly, for Black Lives Matter activism and protests. And "theory" is understood as Marxist obfuscation. Believing predetermines seeing!

No sooner does Rufo take himself to have established the intellectual tradition of CRT – he seems here to mean CRT 1.0 – than he broadens the target. "CRT," he says, "is usually deployed under a series of euphemisms, such as equity, social justice, diversity and inclusion, and socially responsive teaching." There is an obvious political strategy at work here: Renew the longstanding political panic over Marxism and communism, which dates back at least to the McCarthyist 1940s and 1950s, if not to the 1917 Russian Revolution, by embedding this misreading of CRT and CRS as substitutes for its terms. The goal is to set fire to the shift in American politics regarding race and racism, the pace of which had quickened significantly following the George Floyd murder in May 2020. Mark Levin's *American Marxism* bears this out explicitly, as the title makes evident. Out of "CRT" abracadabra the rabbit of Trufism has been drawn magically from the top hat.

*

Rufo is not alone among the Trufer vocalists. There are occasional guest artists doing a star turn. Mark R. Levin is among the most current. Born to Philadelphia Jewish parents, he received both his undergraduate training in Political Science and a law degree from Temple University. He was elected to a school board on a platform to reduce property taxes. Later, he was involved with a law firm for which he worked in targeting the National Association of Education for its political expenditures, before joining the Reagan Administration in the 1980s and became the Chief of Staff for Attorney General Edwin Meese. In 2016 a "Never-Trumper," Levin endorsed Ted Cruz. He increasingly supported Trump during his presidency, eventually becoming a strident Trump supporter. The Trumpian investment expands radio audience and sells books. Levin's constitutional arguments are less secure, regarded by authoritative commentators as not worthy of consideration.[11]

Mark Levin is Rufo's equal for sloppiness. His *American Marxism* sold 700,000 copies in the first three weeks of its publication in summer 2021. In it, and in appearing repeatedly on Fox News to promote the book, Levin pronounced, in keeping with Trufist lines, that CRT "came out of critical theory." He adds that "critical theory," and by extension Critical Race Theory, was "hatched" by "Herbert Marcuse . . . the Hegelian-Marxist political ideologue of the Franklin [sic] school" of "political theorists" founded, he says in live interviews, "in Berlin."[12]

Errors committed by Levin are comparable to Rufo's, if not more embarrassing. The onset of what became known as critical theory was not at the "Franklin School"[13] but the Frankfurt School (even Rufo gets this right) which established itself not in Berlin but, big surprise, at Frankfurt University, in Frankfurt. German cities, all the same.

Levin, to his credit, spends considerable pages quoting Marcuse, especially on "repressive tolerance." What he does almost exclusively is gloss passages he quotes at some length, telling his readers what the passages "actually" say but in ways that invariably render the meaning of the quotes virtually unrecognizable. He begins with a snide passing comment on the concept as a "truly perverse if not bizarre twist on logic and reality,"[14] as if it is inconceivable for tolerance to be

repressive. Levin does acknowledge in passing that the tolerated don't ask to be tolerated. They would rather be recognized
and respected. Tolerance, it has to be emphasized, is always
expressed from a position of (relative) power.[15] Is it such a leap
from an unwanted state to a repressive one?

What Marcuse was concerned to show, not especially con-
troversially, is that a society centering tolerance necessarily,
but less obviously, must have an understanding of its opposite,
of intolerance and repression (shades of Benjamin on civilization and barbarism; that the existence of one relies on the
workings of the other). In place of trying to comprehend (if not
appreciate and socially incorporate) any cultural expression
or behavior that is taken to be alien, tolerance at worst simply
"puts up with it," less directly discouraging the expression in
favor of adopting the host society's dominant social norms.
The violence of the oppressed, Marcuse argues, is invariably
in response to the violence of the oppressor, which, in considering itself legitimate, obscures its own repressive violence
from itself while making it obvious to those it represses. By
dismissing only the reactionary violence of the oppressed as
illegitimate, the violence of the oppressor is simply deepened
and extended.[16] An analysis like Levin's that adopts this strategy extends the relations of power at work: it assumes the voice
of power while enforcing the powerlessness of the alien, the
traditionally repressed.

Even if one took Levin's account of Marcuse uncritically at
face value, there is nothing in the interpretation to support
Rufo's declaration that Marcuse initiated the CRT substitution
of race for class, white for oppressor and Black for oppressed.
This, as I indicated above, is just Rufoistic fabrication. Marcuse
nowhere developed a substantive theory of race, as his peer,
Austrian philosopher Eric Voegelin, did in the early 1930s; or
a theoretical account of racism, as the psychiatrist Magnus
Hirschfeld did in Berlin at the same time; each at considerable
risk to their respective lives.[17]

Levin considers the "nonsensical argument" about "repressive tolerance" the basis of "the Biden administration and Democratic Party," as well as "the media and institutions throughout our culture and society." Those are bald assertions, not an argument or evidence, for which none are offered. He starts the book by insisting that Biden, the Democratic Party, its members of Congress, the "deep state," and much of American mainstream media and academia are Marxist, smitten by its ideology. That the basis of the charge seems to be that they are all committed to "one-party rule," "utopianism," and critical of all things Trumpian makes evident that the Trufist characterization as reductively mischaracterizes Marxism, Democratic politicians, and academics as it does CRT.[18] The silliness undercuts any demand to be taken seriously.

"Critical Race Theory," it turns out for Levin, "is one of the most destructive among these movements."[19] This, I would say, is what is especially nonsensical: In turning to discuss CRT it is readily apparent that Levin himself has consulted next to nothing of it, in any version. He relies exclusively on the work of Trufers. This includes work by Rufo's fellow travelers Butcher and Gonzalez at Heritage, and a little recognized retired political scientist, George LaNoue, whose last scholarly publication of any modest note is nearly thirty years ago (he appears best known for a history of the small college at which he taught).

From Butcher and Gonzalez, Levin ascribes to CRT the suggestion that society is constituted by categories "of oppressor and oppressed"; that "the oppressed" who "adhere to the cultural beliefs of their oppressors" somehow "impede revolution" and must be subjected to "re-education sessions"; that "all societal norms" must be "dismantled . . . through relentless criticism"; and "the replacement of all systems of power . . . and their descriptions" with "a worldview" predicated on "only oppressors and oppressed." From LaNoue, Levin inherits the position that CRT is best represented not by any actual CRT

1.0 thinkers but by who else than "the best-selling proponents Robin DiAngelo and Ibram X. Kendi."[20] The stuck needle of the Trufer broken record. LaNoue is clearly just singing from the Rufo songbook.

Levin concludes that "Marcuse and other Marxists spawned Critical Race Theory and a seemingly endless list of disgruntled, ideologically driven groups."[21] In having his causality backwards Levin reveals two category mistakes bundled together here. The first is that neither CRT nor CRS created disgruntled groups. Disgruntled groups were socially produced by unjust conditions, the grounds for the existence of which CRT and CRS are concerned to analyze and understand. And second, CRT is not an ideology but an analytic, a theoretical practice for revealing and comprehending the socio-racial conditions, their causes and effects constitutive of the disgruntlements at issue. Levin perhaps exemplifies the analytic truism: it is next to impossible to prove an "interpretive negative," in this case that CRT, or Marxism for that matter, didn't do it.

Consider a quote cited by Levin of a 2020 CNN interview with Kimberlé Crenshaw, just as the Trufer attacks on CRT were taking off. Crenshaw made clear that

> Critical race theory attends not only to law's transformative role which is often celebrated, but also to its role in establishing the very rights and privileges that legal reform was set to dismantle. Like American history itself, a proper understanding of the ground upon which we stand requires a balanced assessment, not a simplistic commitment to jingoistic accounts of our nation's past and current dynamics."[22]

Levin's reductive gloss on the quote is that "CRT undermines and exploits America's unique and very successful fusion of diversity and cultural assimilation." He takes Crenshaw to be claiming that CRT considers all issues in the context of past societal imperfections – regardless of enormous struggles and efforts in creating a more perfect society, including a civil war, massive economic redistribution, and groundbreaking legal changes. Even more, it incorporates and advances an increasing list of causes as new or additional reasons for eradicating society and transforming the country. Indeed, CRT repositions what is the most tolerant and beneficent society on earth as a miserably dark and impoverished nation, from its beginning to today.[23]

The contrast, if not unexpected more than a hundred pages into Levin's extensive plastic surgery, is staggering but representative of the complete Trufist make-over. Crenshaw frames her response to CNN by stressing at the outset that "law" has played a "transformative role" in American history. This stands in sharp relief to the sense with which Levin portrays Crenshaw's language as conveying nothing but "a miserably dark and impoverished nation." What CRT 1.0 is concerned to do, Crenshaw adds, is to provide "a balanced" understanding of the complicated role of legal reform in inching toward equality, while helping at the same time to extend the structure of historical and renewed inequalities into the bifurcated country we continue to inhabit. Nuance is to Trufers as truth is to Trump.

Rufo similarly misrepresents Crenshaw. In an interview with Fox News, he thoroughly mischaracterizes the record by dismissing the defenders of CRT as "perpetuating out and out lies," advancing himself as the honest critic. Here he profiles Crenshaw as having "backed away from Critical Race Theory as it is implemented in institutions."[24] Not exactly. Here's what Crenshaw actually said in the *New Yorker* profile about Rufo:

I've been witness to trainings that I thought, Ennnnnh, not quite sure that's the way I would approach it ... sometimes people want a shortcut. They want the one- to two-hour training that

will solve the problem. And it will not solve the problem. And
sometimes it creates a backlash.[25]

This is not "backing away from implementation in institutions."
It is being honestly critical of the way, sometimes, in some
institutions, what represents itself as critical race training is
taken up. Implementation of any theory or policy can fall short
of conception, intention, or aspiration. This is especially so
when those purporting to implement the theory are not those
formulating it. Crenshaw is clear-eyed and honest about the
record. That is far more than one can say about Rufo and his
followers. Is there a single instance where they are self-critical
about their purposeful misrepresentations and failings regarding CRT and the vicious, even violent politics – death threats
to school-board members,[26] hounding principals and teachers
out of jobs for supposedly "teaching" CRT – promoted on the
basis of their misreadings?

Levin charges CRT as identity politics run amock. It is notable, then, that CRT proponents such as Kimberlé Crenshaw
invoke "identity" largely as an object of analysis not embrace.
Social positioning is structurally produced, not reductively a
function of color-coding, as Levin and the like simplistically
presume.

There have been Marxist critics of CRT 1.0 and CRS.[27] This
should give pause to the implication that they are both inherently Marxist, or even derivative from Marxism. That some
practitioners of CRT or CRS are Marxist does not nearly make
all so just as many Republican members of Congress being
Trumpian does not entail all are. Scholarship, especially in the
human sciences, operates by way of point and counter-point.
Projecting absolute consensus among all practitioners of CRT
is like saying all Democrat Congressional members agree on all
points because Republicans insist they do.

The overriding conclusion to reach here is that Trufism
is as intellectually empty as it is morally bankrupt. Trufism

is nothing other than 1950s anti-communism redux. Trump made this explicit in March 2022, at a political rally in South Carolina. "If we allow the Marxists, and communists, and socialists to hate America," he broadcast, "there will be no one left to defend our flag or to protect our great country or its freedom [from Critical Race Theory]." His supporters, he continued, "must lay down their lives" in the fight against "[CRT as] a matter of national survival."[28] That's a tall order to defend against a political phantasm.

The broadside directed at what the CRT critics call "Marxism" takes aim squarely at key terms identified with social justice. Florida Republicans are making significant gains among Latino voters in the state by hammering the message that CRT is a Democratic strategy to turn the country communist, a significant concern for those whose families fled repression in Cuba, Nicaragua, or Venezuela. I will return in Part III to elaborate what the conservative critics seek to achieve politically by this deflection. Rufo and company are concerned to uphold a minimal rhetoric of "equal *opportunity*" while working to resist and erase movement toward more equal racial *outcomes*, economically, politically, and legally, which they reject under the collective banner of "equity." In turn, they either ignore any critical counter to their views or seek to silence them, demonstration of which I now take up.

8

Sounds of Silencing

Rufo's "Briefing Book" outlines a thumbnail sketch of what he takes CRT to be. For Rufo, CRT claims one is "no more than" one's race, and that one will be "*judged*" by "one's *race alone*" (italics in original). "American institutions such as the Constitution and legal system," Rufo continues, "preach freedom and equality, but [for CRT] are mere 'camouflages' for naked racial domination." CRT, apparently then, takes racism to be ubiquitous in the U.S., and so inescapable. It "is a constant, universal condition [for CRT]: it simply becomes more subtle, sophisticated, and insidious over the course of history." One is "destined to fail" because Black, "to be a racist" because white. CRT, Trufers insist, makes white children feel guilty, Black kids that they have no future.

These are all declarations about "Critical Race Theory" Rufo's clones and political chorus, Levin not least among them, have quickly mimicked and loudly circulated. Rufo's materials, his Heritage Foundation and Manhattan Institute's *City Journal* publications, and appearances on Fox News amplify the reach of such pronouncements. They have increasingly found their way into the well-documented public shouting matches at school-board meetings around the country, as well as into the arsenal of right-wing legislators in the U.S., and their imitators in Europe and elsewhere.

Now, following Rufo, Trufers generally think that Robin DiAngelo and Ibram X. Kendi most readily represent CRT thinking. Their book publications have topped or been close to the top of the *New York Times* bestseller lists. Kendi is trained in African American Studies, and DiAngelo is a social psychologist. Neither is a critical race theorist in the classic CRT 1.0 legal mold. Kendi, characterized by CRT's Trufer critics variously as the "critical race guru" or the "New Age guru," has been enormously effective in popularizing some of the critical work on race (though *not* CRT 1.0 work).[1] He has repeatedly insisted he is not a critical race theorist (by which he means CRT 1.0). The Trufist critics seem oblivious to his self-definition, a classic indication at least of racial insensitivity to the concern in Black culture to self-name.

Kendi's work shares little in its theoretical detail with DiAngelo's account of what she famously calls "white fragility." Many contributors to CRT and CRS have pointed out that whites and whiteness may not be nearly as fragile as DiAngelo wants to make out. The itchiness at being called out or losing privilege may as well indicate arrogance rather than fragility. Racial generalizations often tend to devolve into empty ascriptions and stereotypes from all stripes of the political divide. In any case, DiAngelo's "white fragility," an identity characterization, is not a notion readily identified with CRT 1.0.[2] The counter-proposals to combat racism that she offers in her book rely exclusively on demonstrably ineffective personal, individual responses of changing minds and attitudes. They accordingly leave the structural conditions producing the racism she analyzes almost completely untouched. Kendi is a racial structuralist. DiAngelo, by contrast, relies more straightforwardly on agent-centered responses even if nominally acknowledging the impacts of structural racism.

Rufo, then, must badly misread their work to make them fit his charges. DiAngelo's book, *White Fragility*, he suggests, has CRT reducing individuals solely to their race. DiAngelo writes:

> Whiteness is dynamic, relational, and operating at all times and on myriad levels. These processes and practices include basic rights, values, beliefs, perspectives and experiences purported to be commonly shared by all but which are actually only consistently afforded to white people.

Rufo has DiAngelo implying that *only* white people ever benefit in this way. Notwithstanding DiAngelo's serious limitations as a compelling analyst of racism, she is suggesting here that white people *invariably* benefit, while Black people do so at best variably and inconsistently. Even if this is thought too strong in that whites don't always benefit racially, copious evidence makes it clear that whites regularly and generally benefit more readily than Blacks. Pandemic health care and death rates, policing, and access to voting repeatedly bear this out. DiAngelo hardly exemplifies the incendiary radical expression Rufo wants to make it out to be. And, in any case, critiquing "whiteness" does not entail criticism of this or that white person.

For Rufo, CRT is committed to the claim that "All whites are racist." In evidence his Briefing Book adds examples from Kendi. In the quote Rufo attributes to him, Kendi speaks not of whiteness at all but of our "allowing our society to raise [our children] to be racist." This is hardly a controversial position. It is one less about individuals than a cultural system. There are many examples of those raised in a racist home, once able to think for themselves, acting in ways to counter racism. Rufo expresses critical concern about CRT's overgeneralizations. He readily engages in them himself regarding his critical targets.

DiAngelo, like Kendi, is not suggesting that all white individuals are racist but that "[w]hite *identity* is inherently racist," that all whites "exist *within* a system of white supremacy" (my emphases). She clearly means that anyone embracing "white identity" is embracing an identity structured in and benefiting from racism. Those identified as whites, accordingly, can distance themselves by not embracing whiteness, by refusing or distancing themselves so far as possible from its specific benefits. They can speak out in support of racial equality, and engage in action to promote it. DiAngelo obviously could have expressed the point more clearly and carefully. Her position once again reinforces racism as individual expression rather than structural condition, in clear contrast with CRT 1.0. But what she does say, nevertheless, is not nearly as outrageous as Rufo would have it.

There is no doubt that overreaching and wince-worthy racial characterizations have been made, on all sides of the critical racial divide. DiAngelo and, as we will see shortly, Kendi offer their fair share. Christopher Rufo too. In one of his podcast interviews with him, Marc Lamont Hill asked Rufo to name a single affirming characteristic of whiteness he would be happy to embrace. Rufo repeatedly refused to oblige. He reiterated that he prefers people not be judged racially but rather by "their character."[3] For one who demands that whites should not be negatively essentialized, when given the opportunity to identify affirmingly as white and with whiteness, Rufo vacillated. He embraced in its place the established racially structured benefits of "colorblindness," as elaborated in Chapter 6 above.

Two weeks later, Lamont Hill interviewed Liz Wheeler, another conservative "CRT" critic. After incessantly repeating Rufo's obfuscating talking points about CRT's origins in "Marxist Critical Theory," Wheeler pressed Lamont Hill on whether he believed "all whites are racist." Lamont Hill's show was short on time, needing to end with a commercial to pay the bills. He was obviously frustrated, as much by the counter-question as by the endless evasions that Wheeler had pursued through their thirteen-minute back-and-forth. He took a deep breath. And then, instead of saying something like "this is too complicated to respond to in ten seconds, I will have you back," he blurted out, "Yes, I do." He quickly added that "All whites at some level, at the unconscious level, are connected to racism in some ways, that's unavoidable."[4]

Safe behind his social media shield, Rufo tweeted a clip just of Lamont Hill's "I do" response, but nothing of the elaboration.[5] Pronouncing her "gotcha" moment, Wheeler likewise tweeted that Lamont Hill "literally" expresses "a racist ideology."[6] Perhaps turn around is fair play. The right-wing mediaverse had a field day. Lamont Hill, approached by news media outlets, clarified what he really meant: that dominant culture infuses all with elements of racist ideas, including, as he added, himself as a Black person. Rufo, declaring victory, was notably silent about the clarification.[7]

Too often we get caught up in accusing someone of racism, or defending those we otherwise admire from such accusations. Save for repeated egregious individual cases, is it perhaps not better to focus on the structural and systemic conditions underlying racism, to which Lamont Hill was trying to reach, if awkwardly at the outset? Rufo and his followers are clearly more comfortable on the terrain of accusation, with the aim of shutting down, given that they think there is only individual racist expression.

Lamont Hill and Rufo-Wheeler represent polar contrasts regarding racism: broadly systemic and narrowly individualistic, structural and agentive in the terms I delineated in Chapter 3. CRT 1.0 is concerned with keeping focus on the structural and systemic conditions that produce and prolong racism. Confining attention solely to individual charges provides cover for avoiding the larger systemic questions. It narrows racism to at most an exception here or there rather than something socially endemic, pervasive, enduring if not addressed. That Rufo and those he has influenced seek every opportunity to cast aspersions on their critics – look, the accuser is the culprit, the critic of racist ideology is expressing it – provides ample evidence of weaponizing race *as* non-racialism. And of silencing any sustained critique of racism. No country for nuance when it comes to racial matters.

Critical race theorists in the generic sense, including CRS, have often called out racial overreaches by critical colleagues in ways that Rufo-inspired critics never do about themselves. Henry Giroux, a strong CRT/CRS advocate, to take just one example, has pointed out that the sometimes-bald generalizations about whiteness by those engaged in whiteness studies offered white children no affirming sensibilities to which to aspire. This, Giroux argued, has failed to offer possible pathways for white youth into anti-racist engagement.[8] I have seen no single example where Rufo or his supporters criticize each other for overgeneralization, racial misstatement, or misattribution, despite rampant examples of their engaging in such misleading practices.

*

Fabrication operates on two tracks. It works most obviously by fashioning a false account or narrative. Rufo and the Trufers, I indicated above, have cooked the ingredients, passing off poisoned patties for prime cut. But to have a chance at convincing their base, fabrication cannot stop simply at falsifying the terms of the narrative. Fabrication also requires "make-believe," compelling the targeted audience to be invested, to act on the narrative. For Trufers, CRT had to become a compulsion, a knee-jerk response to the fabricating cues. It had to be transformed into something like the Trufist caricature. As the sort of school-board invasions I exemplified in Chapter 1 attest, Rufo's efforts have succeeded beyond Heritage's wildest dreams.

"CRT," Rufo and company bemoan, "promises a utopia" it is completely incapable of achieving. This formulation indicates the Trufist undertaking to turn CRT from an analytic into a political platform. Mainstream European critics have mounted similar charges concerning postcolonial and decolonizing commitments against leading global intellectuals, museums, exhibition and festival curators, and publications.[9] European conservatives have dismissed as unreasonable those calling for repatriation of valuable artworks taken from (former) African colonies, and characterized as nationally insulting those insisting on not erasing colonial histories embedded in cultural heritage. The French philosopher Pierre-André Taguieff goes further, almost comically chiding such critics for expressing "hatred of the West, as a white civilization," as "enemies of European civilization" and "the straight white male," committed to "decolonize, emasculate, de-Europeanize."[10]

Critical Race Theory as Crenshaw and her partners conceived and practice it, nevertheless, is a way of analyzing social conditions, surfacing the otherwise unseen. It is not an institutional apparatus, a set of rules, or even protocols structurally defining an institution. No institutions, whether educational or social, have adopted a platform identified as CRT and committed themselves to institutionalizing it. For one, there is no such identifiable platform. CRT is more like an alarm bell for when things go racially awry.

An honest critique would take concrete issue with (some of) CRT's actual assumptions, logic, conclusions, and their relation, as serious scholarly analysis has done. It would not blame CRT for policies, programs, and practices, or attributed premises and principles it had no actual hand in formulating or implementing. "CRT," a Heritage webinar asserts, collapsing the good and the bad of CRS with CRT 1.0, is "leading to cancel culture." Cancel culture blaming the canceled for "canceling" is the playbook of "fraudit" charging a clean election with fraud. This is the world of the Big Lie.

That opportunist politicians and political fundraising campaigns are using these explicit terms to advance their cause[11] indicates that they think they have struck political gold and are milking the mine for all its worth. Kimberlé Crenshaw and her CRT 1.0 colleagues, unlike the Rufos and Levins, have no personal political aspirations. Their unqualified commitment is to justice, especially for those too often denied it. By contrast, Trufist state legislators have set in place laws enabling individuals to police anything they nebulously identify as CRT circulating in schools, universities, or workplaces, no matter the imploding social terrain they leave in the wake. Anti-LGBTQ+ and anti-abortion mobilizations are being added to the mix. The abiding question is what the racial politics of this political "normalizing" of Trufism represents.

Trufism and the assertion of racelessness codify the radical conservative strategy regarding racism in America and Europe that has gathered steam over the past half-century. The undertaking has been to turn the progressive charge of racism against itself. If institutional and structural racism are things of the past, as Trufers and proponents of racelessness would have it, invoking race to address racism effectively discriminates against *white* people. Anti-racism, so the charge goes, is reverse discrimination. The "new racism" is anti-racism.

The Rufo-influenced extend the criticism to charge CRT with committing to a "new segregation." "CRT," on this view, promotes organizing groups for social activities on racially ascribed lines. Examples are offered of meetings divided strictly into racial groupings or "caucuses," and refusing racial mixture. There are, of course, instances in which students or trainings may be divided in this way, or divide themselves, mostly to provide people of color with "safe spaces" in which to discuss sensitive issues. But can one plausibly generalize to an implication about the whole of CRT or CRS from a relatively small number of exceptions invoked, especially in circumstances where there have been troubling incidents of racism? Where such cases do occur, they are hardly the product of CRT or CRS so much as organizers, administrators, young people, or, most often, diversity trainers seeking to address pressing matters of concern in fraught environments.

Black parents of children attending a Denver school asked school administrators to organize a "families of color playground night." They were interested in establishing a mutual support group and having a chance to discuss their children's experiences at the school. A national anti-CRT group, Parents Defending Education, filed a civil rights complaint to the Department of Education, accusing the meeting of being "immoral and unconstitutional." Mistakes are no doubt made, and statements, especially racially contextualized ones, can come over in awkward ways. This does not mean all such events or expressions are wrong or awkward. No one was precluded from attending the Denver school event, and people from mixed racial backgrounds did. Rufoists tend to turn complex considerations regarding racial issues into simplistic stereotypes of CRT. If the parental meeting is unconstitutional, what of Hillel, Jewish or Christian or gender-specific student organizations on public campuses? Trufism seeks an informal sort of algorithm for alchemically translating CRT into the "Doctrine of Critical Race Theory According to Rufo."

Attributing racism to anti-racism, to racial strategies and practices to address racism, started with the resistance to affirmative action in the early 1970s. These sorts of rejection followed from the commitment to colorblindness. If colorblindness is the standard regarding race in society, any invoking of race for whatever reason, not least when addressing racism, must be racist. Chief Justice John Roberts has commented that "the way to stop discrimination on the basis of race is to stop discriminating on the basis of race."[12] Rufo extends the criticism: "Critical race theorists believe that the state must actively discriminate against racial groups" by way of "racial quotas, race-based benefits," and wealth redistribution.

Just as there has been nearly a half-century of anti-progressive advocacy for this redirection of racism,[13] so there have been vigorous critical discussions and debates in law, politics, and anti-racist theorizing about this strategy of racial reversal. CRT 1.0 has been party to these discussions. Rufo studiously avoids any mention of this. He seems less concerned with a carefully considered exchange of views so much as with a political strategy to damn the critical opposition. And, in the process further to marginalize, effectively to silence critical analysis regarding racism.

Together with the charge of reverse discrimination, Rufo projects that CRT is committed to censoring views about which it is critical, namely, "racist or hateful speech." He implies that this unacceptably constrains the First Amendment, but offers no discussion of the complexities of First Amendment law.

Free speech is legitimately discouraged in all sorts of ways, both as a matter of contextual social practice and in law. The Federal Communications Commission (FCC) restricts the use of curse words and racial epithets on network television or public radio. Art considered insulting to dominant religion has been denied public funding and display. Racist and hateful speech directed at individuals in ways likely to cause a violent reaction has been regulated. Speech can be leading, fighting words disposing to violent outcomes, as storming the Capitol on January 6 demonstrated.

Those Rufo might consider fellow travelers have certainly curtailed speech, notably regarding the use of the term "racism." In the 2021 debate leading up to the passing by the Texas legislature of a controversial bill making it harder for Blacks and Latinos to vote, the House Speaker, Republican Dan Phelan, banned the use of the term "racist." Texas House Democrats objected, maintaining they were characterizing the entire bill as racist, not individual legislators. Phelan overrode the objections, suggesting they could substitute the considerably less critical characterization "racial impact" instead.[14] Censorship cuts both ways.

Once again, Rufo appears to be cheerleading for his followers rather than contributing thoughtfully to a longstanding social debate. Given the sort of public anger exhibited by those fueled by Rufo's ranting about CRT, there may be a range of contexts – school-board meetings, for one – where the public expression of Trufist ideation crosses over from one opinion among others into fighting words.

Rufo's Briefing Book proclaims CRT to be "opposed" to equality under the law and to meritocracy. Rufo and his followers refuse to admit that, in critiquing "equality under the law," critical race theorists are not out to bury legal equality. Rather, their point is to question the way it is structured and implemented in the American legal system. Rights are differentially enforced on grounds of race, class, gender, disability, and their interaction. The legal system demonstrably treats whites, in general, and wealthier white people, especially, more preferably than Black people, notably poorer Black men. Many studies have indicated that the ways drug laws in the U.S. are written up, implemented, enforced, and violations punished have significantly greater impact on Black and Brown people and, by extension, on Black and Brown families, than on whites.[15] This is especially so in cases of comparable violations. A greater proportion of Black than white men convicted of similarly violent crimes has been sentenced to the death penalty. Treating equals equally requires that everyone be relevantly equal from the outset.

Those advocating for CRT 1.0 and CRS seek a fair and just legal and social system, one not racially structured and applied inequitably. And it is not just CRT 1.0 and CRS that have trenchantly critiqued the idea that we live in a meritocracy. Consider, as one example among many, the widely discussed contribution by notable Harvard University philosopher Michael Sandel, who has published nothing notable on racism as such. Sandel thinks a generalized faith in meritocracy has entrenched unjust outcomes in college admissions, reinforcing class, race, and gender unfairness.[16] This in turn reproduces deeply unequal outcomes in access to decent work. Studies have demonstrated that these unequal outcomes result more readily from access to supplementary support in preparing for standardized testing. Affordability for such preparatory workshops is highly correlated with class, race, and culture rather than with individual ability. And the ability to contribute productively to society and profession cannot be reduced only to successful test-taking but requires less recognizable capacities like empathy, social responsibility, a collaborative disposition, and the like.

*

Conservative politicians have contributed actively to the surge of anti-CRT backlash. Senator Josh Hawley of Missouri proposed the "Love America Act"[17] in a Republican bid to cancel the teachings of "Critical Race Theory." Taking his cue from his political godfather while Trump was President, Hawley's proposed bill exhorted physically embracing the flag at every public opportunity, standing hand over heart for the national anthem, and pledging allegiance when told to do so. Appealing to freedom of belief and expression, loving America is being legally mandated – a theatrical imperative – while mandating pandemic masks in the face of a rampaging viral disease and death was being outlawed. A vocal critic and opponent of CRT (he clearly has Rufo's version solely in mind), Hawley proclaimed that his proposed legislation would combat the "misinformation the Left is spreading" that the United States is "a racist country" that is "systemically evil."

"We're a nation of liberators," Hawley declared to Tucker Carlson on the nightly Fox Carlson show. "It's time to reclaim that and to teach our children who we are, who they are, and that's why my bill would say, 'Listen: If a school district gets federal money, you've got to teach the basic truth about the country, [such as] the Constitution, the Bill of Rights, the Declaration, [and] the Pledge of Allegiance ... You've got to replace the lies with the truth, and that's what I'm trying to do'." Public schools in the U.S. already teach all of this, so Hawley's proposed bill does nothing more than prime his conservative base. The "we" and "they" in his advocacy here nevertheless operate on multiple registers, at once conservative and "liberal," generic and racial.

In mid-2021, Arkansas Senator, Tom Cotton, another vocal opponent of the theory, opened an investigation into defense contractor Raytheon's use of training materials that promote "Critical Race Theory." He accused Raytheon's materials of "containing gross stereotypes about various groups, including the racial stereotype that Black people as a group are 'exhausted, frustrated, stressed, barely sleeping, scared, and overwhelmed' ... and white people, Christians, able-bodied individuals, straight people, and English speakers, as members of 'privileged' groups who have 'the luxury to ignore ... injustices.'"[18] Is anyone really saying such things? This reads as parody, proof that racial politics in 2022 remain as politically profitable as they did in 1988 or 1968.

*

There is a good deal Ibram Kendi gets right. He has done much to make far more accessible, not least to youth, central ideas of anti-racism. That's exactly why Trufers target him. But he certainly has made a few unworkable proposals too. One way to fix inequality, he has suggested, is to "pass an anti-racist constitutional amendment." It would "make unconstitutional racial inequity above a certain threshold" and it would "establish a Department of Anti-racism" with "no political appointments."[19] Anti-CRTers have been delighted to stomp on Kendi for these positions. He has made it easier for them to collapse CRS positions into some ill-defined version of CRT. In any case, Kendi gives no indication that he has thought about how virtually impossible it would be to implement his proposal. It operates, however, as a set of unfortunate throwaway statements, much easier to dismiss by Trufers than having to grapple with more carefully crafted analysis of arguments regarding, say, reparations.[20]

In any case, Kendi's suggestion reveals a lack of clarity over how constitutional amendments in the U.S. work, and what they were intended to do. U.S. Constitutional Amendments are famously difficult to pass. They establish general rights for all citizens, as individuals, or lay out very general governing principles and processes, such as those for presidential election and removal. They tend to eschew group rights. The 19th Amendment, for instance, does not explicitly declare a woman's right to vote; it prohibits government from restricting or prohibiting anyone's right to vote on the basis of sex. Constitutional Amendments, in any case definitely do not establish government departments, usually the purview of executive and legislative process. A department has to be funded. The House of Representatives, for example, passed a bill in 2021 to establish an office in the State Department to monitor Islamophobia.

The Fourteenth Amendment does some of what Kendi is proposing, namely, protect individuals from racist behavior toward them – notably *by government*. The U.S. Constitution, notoriously, does not protect groups from targeted expression by racists if not directed at specific persons. Even for hate crime legislation to kick in, there first has to be a targeted criminal wrongdoing against one or more racially identified persons to which the statute adds charges. But for all of that, Kendi's suggestion is a provocation for critical discussion, not an incendiary device to blow up the Republic.

Exhortations to blast the Republic, by contrast, appear much more readily of late to derive from Trufist-leaning supremacist quarters, not from anti-racist advocates. The conservative meme seems to have slipped from "Our country, love it or leave it" to "My country, my way or no way." Covid more than anything has held fire to the feet of those screaming with mob-courage at school-board meetings, "Live free or die."

One can find more substantial disagreements with Kendi. "The only remedy for racist discrimination," he says, "is

antiracist discrimination." So Kendi seems to agree with conservatives that anti-racism is "reverse discrimination." Kendi
thinks such discrimination is legitimate, whereas radical right-
wing policy like Florida's W.O.K.E. Act deems it illegitmate.
But anti-racism is not, or should not be, discriminatory. Giving
person B more of something she has been denied through a
history of racism (an educational opportunity, say) because
person W has had more than his fair share is not discrimination. It undertakes to rectify historical discrimination, to
level the playing field. It is what the neo-Kantian political philosopher John Rawls, not a race theorist of any description,
called "justice as fairness." Kendi adds that "racist institution" is a vaguer concept than his preferred "racist policy."
But institutions can be racist, as the considerable literature on
institutional racism has shown, without having policies that
are, continuing to produce racially exclusionary outcomes
despite having no explicitly racist codes in place. Informal
white managerial networks, for example, might continue to
skew hiring pools and promotions toward whites. Kendi's conceptual focus exclusively on the consequences of *policies* is far
too narrowing.[21]

Kendi doesn't have the depth or range of, say, Cornel West,
but then few do. For all the Trufer focus on Kendi's shortcom-
ings, they nowhere take on West's work (or the substance of
Kendi's, for that matter). They never so much as mention West,
one of the most erudite and persuasive commentators on race
and racism in America. Kendi largely ignores the Trufer mos-
quito buzzing about the ears. With West, Trufers recognize
when they have more than met their match.

*

Making CRT its racial target provides conservatives with a
political object to attack everything identified with race:
arguments, ideals, policies, politics. Rufo and crew proceed
by conceptual "collapsology," a logic of conceptual collapse.
All criticisms of racism, diversity, equity, etc. are collapsed

into "CRT" in order to reject them all with a single strike and next to no argument. A similar criticism can be leveled against European conservatives taking aim, in the name of non-racialism, at anti-racist initiatives or pedagogical developments like decolonization.

Take James A. Lindsay, "mathematician, apolitical, for freedom," and rampant tweeter. "@ConceptualJames" posted a page from a published article, which he simply dismissed with the remark, "Critical Race Theory is insane." Admittedly, the page posted – no author named – is the sort of jargon-filled writing too often characteristic of 1990s academic analysis, and close to indecipherable. But there is no reference on the page tweeted to CRT but to CLS – Critical Legal Studies – which CRT 1.0 emerged to counter.[22] ConceptualJames, like his Rufoistic fellow travelers, practices conceptual collapse. This is hardly the virtue of clear-minded thinking to which he apparently subscribes. And these sorts of collapsed attributions are made by appealing to racelessness.

Legal analysts such as Bell and Crenshaw, in short, are committed to surfacing how racism is structured into the social system, in order to address the injustices this continues to produce. The counter-story Rufo and his fellow travelers spin is that racism is not systemic or structural but the product of occasional individual behavior. On this telling, both the expression of conventional racism and how its targets respond are matters solely of personal agency and responsibility. The country effectively has or should have moved on from and, perhaps, at worst, washed its hands of any grappling with socially embedded racism and its legacies.

*

I elaborate in Part III how the line of critical attack projected by Rufo's drum-beating and those it influences has re-energized the racial politics of racelessness. Rufo has sought to ascribe racism to those critical of racism. In implying that CRT advocates are seeking to silence commitments to colorblind equality, Trufers have been looking to shut down all critical targeting of structural racism that continues to benefit whites. The question is whether, in doing so, they are whitewashing the politics of race once again.

Part III

The Politics of "CRT"

9

Deregulating Racism

The 1960s represented possibility, a significant push to open up even in the face of intense violence and danger. Law played a crucial role. The 1964 Civil Rights and 1965 Voting Rights Acts advanced at least formal equality, while keeping alive the question of substantive equality. The stepping-stone of affirmative action in college admissions and hiring became more readily if far from universally institutionalized. Anti-colonial independence movements gathered momentum with a run of hard-won victories. Student and cultural movements sought to break with the constraints of parents and pasts.

By the late 1960s and early 1970s, hopes seemed dashed. Legal challenges to race-based admissions and hiring were increasingly being mounted. In Britain Enoch Powell delivered an infamous speech declaring that due to the surge of Black and Brown immigration "I am filled with foreboding; like the Roman, I seem to see the River Tiber foaming with much blood." The attendant "discrimination and deprivation," he fumed, was suffered not by the immigrant but their drowning white hosts. Immigration should be cut off completely, he concluded, and those already present encouraged to "re-emigrate."

Powell's speech presaged the onset of an even less hospi-
table turn, and far from only in Britain. Though 11 percent of
U.S. troops in Vietnam after the Civil Rights Act was passed
in 1964, Blacks constituted just two percent of the officer
corps and suffered twice the rate of casualties as white troops.
Where colonialism had invested heavily in maintaining colonial bureaucracies on the ground, independence was followed
by neocolonial logics of economic and proxy political control.
Anticipation and possibility became more tempered. This was a
turn(ing back) Derrick Bell's prescient legal and fictional work
on the invariable slippages of racial reform was registering
earlier than most. It is against this backdrop that the general
critical discussion of race and racism, outlined in Chapter 3,
ramped up toward the end of the 1970s and into the 1980s.

Attacks on affirmative action in the U.S. were joined by the
targeting of a stridently stereotyped Black culture in the 1980s
("thug life," "welfare queens," "crack heads"). Policing and surveillance of Black neighborhoods in larger cities intensified,
fueled by the crack epidemic. As President, Ronald Reagan
sought to undermine affirmative action, embracing its redefi-
nition as "reverse discrimination" popularized by *Bakke v. the
University of California* (1978). He further deployed Edwin
Meese's Justice Department (whose Chief of Staff, recall, was
Mark Levin) to curtail, if not completely decimate, civil rights
legislation. Incarceration especially of young Black men began
to spiral. Reagan's efforts were extended by George H.W. Bush
as exemplified in a key campaign commercial notoriously
deployed against Michael Dukakis in the 1988 Presidential election. Willie Horton was a convicted murderer in Massachusetts.
On a weekend furlough outing defended by then Governor
Dukakis, Horton raped a woman after assaulting her fiancé.
Bush's campaign ad showed a shadowy Horton circling repeatedly through a revolving prison gate. It baldly suggested the
inevitability of recidivist crimes by convicted Black men enjoy-
ing soft-on-crime progressive policies. Bill Clinton expanded

criminalization, with racially differential impact. Here was the playbook the Trump administration inherited decades later. As President, Trump doubled down on these commitments, seeking to roll back even the modest advances in racial justice that had been achieved under President Obama.

Trump surrounded himself with those all too ready to curtail civil rights, from Steve Bannon to Attorney General Jeff Sessions and their protégé Stephen Miller, who served as President Trump's senior advisor for policy and White House director of speechwriting. Trump had hinted at the racial politics defining his governing logic, coming to the Presidency by using Cambridge Analytica to purposefully depress the Black vote. Drawing on personal profiles secreted from Facebook, political advertising was directed at African-American voters discouraging them from showing up at the polls. Upon assuming office, Trump was quick to limit immigration especially of Muslims and those of African descent.

When raised expectations appear dashed, a mix of resentment and resistance is likely to be prompted. For Black and Brown people, the at best uneven record on formal equality spotlighted the large legacy of substantive inequality structurally reproduced in society. A UCLA study found in 2014 that once again a rising majority of Black and Latino students was attending underfunded "minority–majority" schools across the U.S.[1] It was the legal structures, processes, and impacts making such reproduced inequalities possible, if not likely, that CRT 1.0 was formulated by Crenshaw and her colleagues to address. In the process, it put aside resentment in favor of incisive socio-legal analysis and substantive transformation.

Racism remains endemic to society and (a considerable range of) its social structures. This is not to say, as Trufers determine CRT does, that racism is so constitutive of America that there is no hope of undoing it or its legacies of effect. Derrick Bell's skepticism notwithstanding, he had a lifelong commitment to fighting for racial equality, as has his former student, Kimberlé Crenshaw and her colleagues. CRT in the broad emerged as a commitment precisely to addressing equitable legal and social advancement on racial matters, not least in the face of their curtailment.

*

By mid-2020, the ceaseless reports of police brutality and killings across the U.S. had focused national attention on anti-blackness. The deadly violence energized anti-racist protests and struggles, exploding with the public police execution of George Floyd in Minneapolis. Used to not having to think much about racism, whites were confronted on a daily basis about the social arrangements racism had helped substantially to create for them. Whites had lost control of the narrative over which they had almost always exercised defining power, more-or-less unthinkingly, and which those invested in the affordances of whiteness were at a loss living without. Trump's presidency only sharpened the dilemma and drama. Trufism emerged as the counter to the counter.

The now unvarnished truth of racism, the worlds it had created, the advantages and disadvantages, the relative risks to life, were no longer deniable. The old order had become unsettled. The anxieties accompanying the loss of overriding control manifested in multiple forms. That the truth was undeniably present, the realities so evident, could only mean that the counter to the counter would end up manifesting as nothing but make-believe. Compulsive fabrication became the demand of the day. The invention of Trufism was the offering on order. That it took the form it did was pretty much baked into the siren song.[2]

CRT 1.0, to be clear, is not Rufo's real target. It is not just CRS. Rufo and his supporters have taken aim at the more readily dismissible expressions and practices they identify as being done by "CRT" as such. Make the "shocking" and "horrifying" the "clear political villain," as RealChrisRufo has explicitly proclaimed, and generalize that to include all of anti-racism.

Rufo and company are consumed with using whatever incendiary statements they "find," if not concoct, to blow up all critiques of racism under the banner of "CRT" as a whole.

We have all said some silly and outrageous things, especially when younger, that we might want to take back. Trufers are no exception. Overgeneralizations, race-explicit and colorblind, abound across the divides. But they far from exhaust critical insight and concern. Trufers are super-quick, in terms of their CRT fabulation, to decontextualize, de-mean, and misconstrue otherwise trenchant criticism by race analysts.

Legal scholar Patricia Williams's metaphor that racism has the impact of "spirit-murdering" its targets, squeezing out of them the will to exist, is hardly untrue. It is what incessant racism does. It snuffs out the flame of spirit. The notion has drawn scornful howls of Rufo-driven outrage. Jason Hill's literal and contestable suggestion (published in *The Federalist*, no less) that "CRT *aims* to murder the souls of white children" – the charge of an intentional violent act against minors printed in *the* major conservative public legal outlet, no less – registers nary a raised eyebrow among the converted.[3]

Rufo and his followers offer a slew of embarrassing examples they ascribe to "CRT." These tend to have been culled from diversity and inclusion training materials by "racial experts" or curricula plans for school teachers, government agencies, and corporate workplaces. Some examples indeed may be wince-worthy, as Crenshaw noted earlier. The Trufer suggestion, however, seems to be that because such workshops are presuming to inculcate principles of social equity, diversity, and social justice, they must be instances of "Critical Race Theory."

There is a tradition of these sorts of "racial expert" training, from civil rights advocacy to multiculturalism and diversity training in the 1990s, to "Diversity, Equity, and Inclusion" (DEI) programs today.[4] A good deal of such materials and their application derive from undertakings by people who have joined the thirty-year bandwagon of consultants and trainers, responding to marketplace demand and charging a tidy sum. In the 1990s, for example, considerable criticism was mounted from race-critical observers and multiple books were published on the subject concerning "corporate multi-culturalism." This was the undertaking, rather reductively and flatly, to apply the thought-provoking principles of critical multiculturalism to corporate, NGO, or university workplace issues, often by well-meaning but less than well-prepared or theoretically nuanced people. Like DiAngelo, they more often than not address structural conditions with solutions set at the level of individual relations and interactions (DiAngelo's latest book, *Nice Racism*, bears this out).[5] These efforts faced similarly vehement pushback from right-wing interests at the time. Nobody, however, thought these activities the product reductively of CRT.

It is true that "anti-racism" has been turned partly into something of an industry. But "diversity training," "racial equity," "systemic" and institutional racism," and indeed "anti-racism" are not derivative from CRT, and all but "diversity training" among these terms pre-date it. Everyone, even the Trufers, are all for "diversity." Rufo's Briefing Book explicitly exhorts his followers to advocate at school-board meetings for "diversity without division." But diversity without division is like a curry without the curry powder. Contestation comes with the turf. Otherwise it is called assimilation. And assimilation is notoriously one-sided, forcing the assimilated to leave behind who they are. Sooner or later that grates. The point is to work together through the division creatively and respectfully, not to bury it alive. As my wonderful colleague and dear friend, the Kenyan writer Ngũgĩ wa Thiong'o puts it, "Culture comes from messiness. It never comes from the neat."

Like "diversity" over the past decade and "multiculturalism" before that, "critical race theory" is being made the barrow carrying the baggage accompanying criticism of racism. The foolishness sometimes said and done in CRT's name nevertheless is being used as a sledgehammer to bash any-thing identifiable as critical of racism and the practices that perpetuate it, no matter how trenchant. "Diversity, Equity, and Inclusion" is the institutional iteration adopted to address their institutional lacks in education, government, and the pri-vate sector as America especially but far from only has grown increasingly heterogeneous. The DEI commitment emerged as affirmative action came increasingly under attack. It doesn't owe its existence to CRT. DEI would have materialized anyway without any reference to the theory.

"CRT" has quickly replaced "political correctness" as con-servatives' generalized target of opportunity. It is more readily identifiable than the latter, which seems more nebulous. It appears to have a definitive referent, and a history. It is being painted with the brush of "socialism" and "Marxism," the sure-fire means to parodic dismissal.

*

The second half of Rufo's Briefing Book offers a playbook for anti-CRT activism. Rufo sets out to provide the anti-anti-racism crusade its drum beat terms by which CRT, or any account critical of racism in America's past and present, is to be publicly demonized. He divides these tactics into three types: negatively defining CRT; attacking CRT in schools; and advocating for anti-CRT legislation.

The first undertaking to color the target negatively frames CRT in terms we have come to expect from the Trufers, including "race-based Marxism," "woke racism," and "racial engineering."[6] Rufo's list characterizes CRT as seeking to face "past discrimination" with its own version of "present discrim-ination" (this is Rufo paraphrasing the nearly fifty-year charge of "reverse discrimination," and Kendi's insistence on "anti-racist discrimination" is his fuel). But he adds make-believe representations even more extreme. Rufo wants all to think that for CRT "individualism, rationality, and hard work are racist." This battle cry is in fact code for a prevailing stereotype about Black intellectual incapacity and laziness. In short, a stereotype of a stereotype. If Rufo has "done a study" here, who, exactly, advocates this, and where is any such claim explicitly to be found?

In the past year, the Coliseum of race struggles in America has been shifted back from the streets and squares of public life to public schools, their districts, and school boards. Schools have been a centerpiece of the fight over racial futures. A racial focus on students has increasingly marked European societies too, as the range of experiences in France, the Netherlands, Britain, Sweden, and, at the extreme, Breivik in Norway[7] all bear out. Schools define for the next generation how to think about historical memory and approach social arrangement. In the U.S. these struggles have ranged from at least *Brown v. Board* (1954) to school desegregation efforts, busing to affirmative action. And of late the fight over CRT and the 1619 Project.

Trufers obviously now assume public schools as their main target. Jonathan Butcher's more recent book, following Rufo's lead, insists that "Critical race theory has hijacked the U.S. education system on every level."[8] This targeting was never a given, and the surge in Rufo-inspired activism around CRT and schooling caught much of the political class by surprise, as it has the rest of us. The folks at Heritage, however, by late 2020 already had schools in their sights, perhaps the result of Butcher's expertise and experience.

The attacks on CRT ramped up while children were at home on Covid lockdown. Middle- and upper-middle-class white mothers were primed by Rufo-rhetoric to see in lesson plans insidious racial design. In the past they didn't much have to think about race. It was the taken-for-granted, the unspoken presumption of place and standing in the inherited socio-racial order. Reflected and reproduced in the educational materials of their own schooling, they fully expected to find these presumptions in those of their kids. Now their own living rooms were being turned into spaces of racial contestation. If there is one thing white parents see in common when concerned about their children being corrupted by rap music, BLM street protests, and the 1619 Project, it has to be the specter of race. CRT, or Rufo's account of it, has been made both fuel and cipher for these paranoid concerns.

Rufo's Briefing Book has clearly been revised to reflect this surge, promoting key terminology to be used in targeting schools, administrators, and boards. "CRT," the Book urges, amounts to "re-education programs" (obviously playing, disparagingly, on identification with Soviet and Chinese communisms). Teachers invoking open-endedly defined CRT in classes are to be vilified as "political predators" and "indoctrinators." Children, the Briefing Book writes in language widely circulated by Rufo's supporters, are being taught that they are "defined by their race, not as individuals." And a slogan that also has come to be mimicked as widely by Rufo's followers as by politicians like Governor DeSantis: "CRT" educates children "to hate each other and hate their country." The cynicism runs deep.

Ketanji Brown Jackson was nominated by President Biden in 2022 to be the first Black woman U.S. Supreme Court Justice. At her Senate Judiciary Committee hearing, Senator Ted Cruz attacked her for sitting on the board of Georgetown Day School, a noted private school in Washington DC. (Thurgood Marshall once also sat on the school board.) The school, Cruz vented while waving at Judge Brown books like Kendi's *Antiracist Baby*, one he had accused the school of keeping in its library, "teaches Critical Race Theory." When Brown responded by rehearsing the history of the school's founding in 1945 by six white Jewish and Black families wanting their children to attend school together in the still school-segregated city, Cruz interjected, "Okay, so you agree critical race theory is taught at Georgetown Day School." Fox News headlined their reporting that "Jackson serves on board of school that promotes critical race theory," and the Republican National

Committee retweeted an image of the Judge with her initials "KBJ" struck out and replaced by "CRT." For the likes of Cruz, Rufo's anti-CRT fabrication is licensing the erasure of the history of desegregating schools.

The drive to erase uncomfortable histories is common to nationalist commitments to authoritarianism. With the onset of Putin's invasion of Ukraine, a major exhibition about the history of the Soviet Gulag in Moscow was closed down, at the very moment Putin was having protestors arrested, all independent media shuttered, and Ukrainian citizens shipped to Russian "reorientation" camps. Nationalist historical revisions, joined with undertakings to constrain free elections, have been pursued similarly in Orbán's Hungary and Modi's Hindutva India. It was a defining feature of South Africa's apartheid state.

As numerous commentators have observed, if you want to move people to action, target their children. That, of course, is part of it. But Trump had already fueled his followers in incendiary fashion. They were looking for ways to have impact, poised to jump in. For some, January 6 was that moment. Schools, however, are local, familiar, within reach, and vulnerable. That the Trufist charges are completely baseless is beside the point. The storming of schools is to control the educational agenda, and in doing so to help produce the Trumpetarians of the future.

Hillsdale College is a small ultra-conservative institution in rural Michigan, leading the charge to recast public schooling by replacing public schools with state-funded charters based on a redefined curriculum. Hillsdale takes no federal funding so it can avoid any government regulation. Its long-serving President, Larry Arnn, was a co-founder of the conservative think tank, Claremont Institute, and he has served as a trustee of the Heritage Foundation for the past two decades. Rufo has spoken at the college, and published in its magazine. Revealingly, the magazine in the past has characterized Putin, a former, hardly reformed KGB official, as "a hero to populist conservatives around the world." The Hillsdale curriculum trains teachers in "the classical tradition," centralizes "the Western curriculum," while defining the U.S. as "an exceptionally good country." It excoriates affirmative action as well as the New Deal and Great Society. Tennessee's state Governor contracted Hillsdale to create fifty new charter schools. Charter schools are publicly funded but privately run. More than $30 million in state public tax funds for education are being redirected for the cause.

The effect of Hillsdale schools is to deepen school segregation, purge the curriculum of any "progressive" lesson modules, and replace "leftist academic" teachers by Hillsdale graduates. Tennessee exemplifies a wider pattern being elaborated nationally: in addition to the Tennessee contract, they have 42 schools running across numerous Republican-led states. Located in more rural and upper income suburbia, Hillsdale school student bodies are whiter than local urban public schools. In a suburban Atlanta Hillsdale charter, the student body is 71 percent white where local public-school populations are just 17 percent so. Student SAT scores are higher than the national average, achieved, however, by expelling struggling students before the tests are taken. In Spring 2021, twelve Black students were dismissed right before test-taking season.[9] To be fair, though, after Arnn insulted public school teachers as ill-prepared and seeking to steep schoolchildren in leftist propaganda, Republican lawmakers in Tennessee have sought, so far unsuccessfully, to scrap the Governor's contract with Hillsdale.

The politics underlying the Tennessee Governor's solicitation of Hillsdale College is nevertheless discernible in one public school district experience in his state. An irate white parent objected to the inclusion in the curriculum of a book about Ruby Bridges' experience as the first Black student to integrate New Orleans schools in 1960.[10] The Tennessee parent declared Bridges' portrayal hurtful to white learners like her child. Ruby's account describes a "large crowd of angry white people who didn't want Black children in a white school." The Tennessee parent determined it was too harsh, pointing out that it offered "no redemption" for white children. She reportedly objected also to another book about school segregation history, expressing disapproval of teaching words like "injustice" and "inequality" in "grammar lessons."[11]

This parent is clearly seeking to produce children who, like many parents, comprehend nothing of how the U.S. has been shaped. It takes just a click on the keyboard to find a clip of what Ruby Bridges had to endure.[12] But it would clearly take a good deal more to come to terms with the experience of a six-year-old girl being screamed at by a crowd of angry white adults and teenagers, the predecessors of this parent, spitting, cussing, screaming, and stone-throwing at her as she sought simply to attend school. (One might read this for our time also as wanting to attend school without likely being infected by another deadly disease.) As Ruby entered the otherwise white school, the white teachers and children fled, refusing to return. Just one teacher remained, committing for the remainder of the year to giving Ruby Bridges the education she sought and deserved. This was not white redemption but the courage of an anti-racist teacher in 1960 New Orleans, no less, committed to matching the resilience of a six-year-old.

Trufism can offer no comparable lesson precisely because it has nothing closely resembling this kind of life-forming experience. In September 2021, a group of white high-school students in Kansas City circulated a petition among their fellow students (about two-thirds in the district are white) calling for slavery's reinstatement. The deafening silence regarding this case by those storming school-board meetings across the country is telling, even unsurprising. A 2021 poll has 43 percent of Republicans wanting *no* teaching of the history of racism (which would include slavery) in public schools.[13] Perhaps returning to early nineteenth-century American history textbooks in which slavery received no mention[14] is what, for them, it means to "make America great again."[15]

In Traverse City, Michigan, an all-but-white town evenly politically split, white high-school students ran a Snapchat group they called "slave trade." They used it to auction students of color in their school. One participant messaged "all Blacks should die" and "let's start another holocaust" (making evident the way in which anti-Black racism and anti-Semitism reinforce each other, as both Jean-Paul Sartre and Frantz Fanon had pointed out already in the 1950s). In the ensuing fallout, school district administrators tried fast-tracking an equity resolution condemning racism. A small group of parents, denying any attention to race, forced erasure of resolution language condemning "racism" and "racial violence," or declaring that "racism and hate have no place in our schools or in our society," or calling for subjecting the curriculum to a "social equity and diversity lens." Other language cuts included encouragement to add "marginalized" authors to their libraries, and that students should learn more about "diversity, equity, inclusion, and belonging issues."[16] Bigoted adults in a bigoted culture tend to reproduce bigoted offspring.

The Free to Learn Coalition is a "non-partisan" Trufist organization committed to "taking politics out of school."[17] The organization launched with $700,000 in funding, intending a million-dollar plus national campaign to "take on activist school boards and administrators." They demand that children should be able to learn and question free from pressure or requirements – fair enough – "to subscribe to a singular worldview" (by which they clearly intend, without explicitly naming, CRT). It is not the singularity to which they object; it is that the worldview is not theirs.

The Coalition's first act was to take out a $500,000 commercial buy on national television to recall the school board in Loudon County, Virginia. This is operationalizing conservative leadership's plan for Republican takeover of American politics from the ground up. It started during Trump's presidency. Ultra-conservative judges were appointed to the courts. The energy has shifted to seizing control of public-school districts. The work is being funded by billionaire dark money.

No sooner had this campaign launched, in September 2021, than Rufo-inspired activists took aim at a related set of targets, in ways deeply revealing of their mode of execution. In early October 2021, the National School Board Association (NSBA) issued a letter requesting that Attorney General Merrick Garland investigate those *violently* targeting school boards and teachers. The NSBA implored the Department of Justice, when warranted, to define such acts as cases of "domestic terrorism" so as to support the most serious criminal charges when lives are threatened. Garland publicly issued a request to the FBI to investigate such "threats to public servants," about which there has been much journalistic reporting, to ensure their ongoing "safety."

Within minutes of Garland's letter going public, Rufo tweeted a copy of the first few paragraphs, under his pronouncement that "Garland has instructed the FBI to mobilize against parents who mobilize against critical race theory in public schools, citing 'threats'." Notice the translation from the legitimate concern about the safety of targeted public-school personnel into the terrorizing of parents concerned about "CRT." (Three months later, a school superintendent, her staff, and their families in California were receiving daily death threats for investigating white students who had painted swastikas on their torsos at a house party.) There is no mention of parents or CRT in either the NSBA or Garland letters. The focus is a legitimate concern with possible and documented violence. The violence has far from all been conducted by parents but by visibly violent political activists. These activists often have no other associations with the school or district. Their targets are people trying to do their jobs serving the public.

Senator Tom Cotton quickly retweeted Rufo under his own declaration that "Parents are speaking out against Critical Race Theory in schools. Now the Biden administration is cracking down on dissent."[18] Senator Josh Hawley soon followed suit, "tearing into Garland for FBI crackdown on alleged harassment of school officials" (as reported by – you guessed it – Fox News),[19] later calling for Garland's resignation. Fox News followed almost instantaneously with a report that the FBI is conducting a (non-required) training on "intersectionality" for its employees.[20] Fox was alerted to the story by – who would know? – Christopher Rufo. As if there is something insidious, as Joint Chiefs of Staff Chairman General Mark Milley put it in his own Congressional hearing, with trying to understand why people are angry.

This extended example reveals the Trufist operation in real time. A legitimate concern about the wellbeing of public servants is turned by Rufo into a "Critical Race Theory" moment. Senators renowned for blowing up CRT for political purpose join the chorus. Fox News enlarges the political detonation by leading with it on their evening news feeds. "CRT" once more is made the medium for political attacks regarding concerns with which it actually has nothing to do. Trufism 101.

So, politics is pursued expansively, loudly, and expensively to prohibit supposed politics, the other's, in school. The politics of a curriculum defined by conservative white parents and racist activism by their children apparently is universal truth, even if representing a shrinking minority. Anything critical of that approved curriculum or deviating from it is rejected as unacceptably "political." Racisms are unleashed against their traditional targets, by undertaking to regulate the supposedly "new" racism – against whites.

*

That Trufism has taken hold of the right-wing imagination reflects the jaundiced filter through which Trumpian influence has blurred how social relations are to be viewed. The majority white American population has been shaped to expect racial standing in the society they have historically taken themselves to enjoy. In the past couple of decades this expectation – a sense of self-entitlement – has grown increasingly shaky, if not illusory. The pandemic and hastening environmental threats have only thrown the concerns into sharper relief.

These socio-economic challenges, as they often do when intensified, have assumed a more visceral turn. And unsurprisingly this tends to take on racial expression. Two decades ago, white Americans made up more than 70 percent of the population. Ten years on that proportion had slipped to almost 66 percent. Over this past decade the slide has only accelerated, and currently whites constitute less than 58 percent. By 2040, the country as a whole will look like California, with a plurality and no racially identified majority. This was not unpredictable, given that those regarded as racially "European" or white constitute roughly 11 percent of global demography. As in Europe, the white birth rate has slowed and reversed. At the very least, it significantly lags the African, Asian, Middle Eastern, and mixed-race heritage birth rate. The United States and Europe cannot keep up with their own employment demands, at all registers of economic and social need. In the age of interactive global movement, the global North is just catching up with how the planet at large looks and its varieties of thinking and culture.

With these demographic shifts, too, more racially diverse people are now teachers in schools and colleges. They hold positions in economic and political life that have diversified interests, commitments, and cultural representation. The accounts of U.S. and European history and culture are not as streamlined as they were long taken to be.[21] This is a predictable product of global demographic, environmental, and political forces, not some insidiously intended "replacement" scheme.

Tucker Carlson, who is arguably the most highly watched political opinionator and influencer on American television, invoked the "great replacement theory" popular among white supremacists to diss these trends. The concept was originally coined by a French writer, Renaud Camus, concerned like Enoch Powell in Britain about France's characteristic "villages" being overrun by immigrants, rendering them all too "unFrench." The Democrats, Carlson complained, are out to deplete the proportion of whites in America, supporting "nonwhite" immigrants as a way to secure electoral majorities. Carlson's quick uptake of the replacement drum exemplifies the transnational movement of ideas, influence, and impact. Facing criticism and calls for Fox to fire him, not least from the head of the Anti-Defamation League (the white supremacist basis of "Great Replacement" has older anti-Semitic roots), Carlson dug in and embraced the criticism on a radio interview with his former Fox colleague, Megyn Kelly.[22] A large national poll in December 2021, a *real* study in contrast to any of Rufo's, found that 45 percent of Republicans (30 percent of American adults overall) believe that immigrants are coming to the U.S. to replace "native-born" citizens, and (in slightly lesser percentages) to influence the outcome of American elections to favor Democrats (which, they think in any case discriminate against whites). These ratios correlate with those watching right-wing news channels like Fox.[23]

The "great replacement theory" with its claims of accelerated immigration and demographic diversification is now being more broadly invoked. For example, the head of the national border patrol union charged the Biden administration with seeking to "weaken the southern border" so as to "change the demographics of the electorate" in order "to stay in power." The theory is hardly benign. Its history of explicitly motivating violence since Trump assumed the presidency in 2017, includes a string of murderous events: the Charlottesville, Virginia white supremacy "Unite the Right Rally" that resulted in one killing (2017); the Walmart shooting in El Paso that killed twenty-two (2019); the Christchurch, New Zealand mosques rampage that murdered fifty-one (2019); the Pittsburgh and Poway, San Diego synagogue shootings killing eleven and one respectively (2018 and 2019); and the supermarket shooting in Buffalo, New York that hit thirteen Black people, killing ten (2022). The shooters all had posted about "invasion" or "replacement," whether by Jews, Muslims, Mexicans, or Blacks. The pandemic-related surge in violence against Asians can be linked to replacement paranoia too. A manifesto published by the eighteen-year-old killer in the Buffalo case also explicitly castigated CRT. And ultra-conservative Wisconsin Senator, Ron Johnson, baselessly blamed "CRT" and "wokeness" for prompting the Texas school shooting in May 2022, killing nineteen children and two teachers. The message is the mantra.

Towns that were once overwhelmingly white are fast changing. Take Southlake, an affluent suburb of Dallas-Forth Worth. In the past twenty years the white majority has dropped from 80 percent to about 60 percent. As the town has grown more heterogeneous, conflicts and tensions have dramatically increased, not least around expectations at the high school. White students have expressed themselves in racially insensitive ways. When the school district tried, in response, to institute diversity initiatives, white parents increasingly turned to Rufo-inspired talking points at school-board meetings. Southlake, presumptively ruled by and for whites, no longer seemed to its self-presumed landlords to be properly, uncontestedly Texan.[24]

White residents, formerly not having to think about the changes it takes to live in a diverse country, want the rules they expect to advantage them not to have to alter. "We didn't have to think about racism then; we don't want to have to think about it now. Yesterday we could be racist with impunity; we don't want to be held accountable, for what we did or said then, do or say today." And lack of accountability means remaining in control of the levers of power.[25] The tension is only heightened by the fact that the more diverse segments of the population tend to be younger, have trended significantly less politically conservative, especially at higher education levels, and are less likely to vote for Republican candidates. Nearly 60 percent of college attendees (and a college degree is still strongly correlated with higher lifetime earnings) are women. The numbers alone portend a Republican, and especially white male, political wilderness.

In the face of these fast-shifting trends, refusal and denial appear to have become the default fallback mode of hyper-conservativisms. By definition, conservativisms take their cue retrospectively, seeking to conserve a "heritage," invariably partial and restrictive. In any case, "Mak[ing] America Great Again" draws on a narrowed romanticized retrospective of what the U.S. was as the model for what it should be. A self-elevated talk show host implored Black fans to leave country music alone as they "have their own music" in hip hop and the blues. Even music fandom should revert to its previously segregated state. Johnson Cash is groaning from his grave.

The quicker the pace of change, the more assertive and insistent the reach for the idealized moment of imagined past control and privilege. From 1948 to 1994, South Africa lived under formal apartheid. This was a Christian nationalist regime headed by white men, the state conceived to embody a religious vision. The state institutionalized structural and systemic racism. Almost only whites could vote, legally own guns and most did, abortion and homosexuality were banned, education was reinforced state propaganda. What we appear to be witnessing today in real time in the U.S. is the reach for a "raceless" updating of this mode of white minority rule. Hungary's Orbán, a model for conservative America, made this explicit in a public address in July 2022. "One half is a world where European and non-European peoples live together," Orbán declared. "These countries are no longer nations. They are nothing more than a conglomeration of peoples. . . . We do not want to become peoples of mixed race."[26] "Don't worry," he gleefully told the annual American conservative CPAC conference in 2022 a week later, "Christian politicians cannot be racist."

It turns out that the bellicose political resistance to diversity efforts in Southlake, Texas, was not quite as innocent as it seems on the surface. Patriot Mobile is a young start-up mobile company active in the suburbs around Dallas. It brands itself as committed to "making America Christian again" and, as the company name suggests, to reigniting patriotic American nationalism. Its CEO and senior management, all white, are committed to using the company's profits to instill its expressed conservative Christian values more broadly. CEO Leigh Wambsganss, a longtime political activist, mobilized white parents in Southlake to resist the bubbling changes. Believers in the newish religious doctrine of Dominionism, Patriot Mobile calls for institutionalizing that doctrine's core commitments: Christian takeover of government, business, media, and education. Ted Cruz's father, a well-known Texas pastor, runs weekly prayer meetings at the company's headquarters. In 2021 the company's political action committee donated over $500,000 to support school-board candidates in the area, including Southlake's, and in 2022 tripled their donations. The candidates they support, all white Christian nationalists, prevailed in taking over four area school boards. As board members they have already moved to delimit school teaching about race and gender, restrict student use of pronouns to their traditional binaries, and remove from schools books they deem unChristian. Their stated intention is to expand their political reach, both in Texas and other southern states such as Florida.[27]

Besides its bellicosity, however, this apparent re-institutionalization of white rule is predicated on an underbelly of anxiety, too. A poll by Larry Sabato at the University of Virginia found that, among those voting for Trump in 2020, 84 percent expressed growing concern with rising "anti-*white* discrimination" (accompanied by concerns about the future for Christianity in the country).[28] The vast majority of those who showed up at and many of whom stormed the U.S. Capitol on January 6, 2021 to declare Trump won the Presidential election live in counties scattered across the nation that have diminishing white majorities. White voters have tended to support Republicans by a little more than 10 percent than they do Democrats. The gap is significantly wider for white Christian and less urban voters, ranging from Catholics (15 percent more) to evangelicals (69 percent more) and rural whites (over 40 percent more). Trufism is the tail wagging the dog barking for its masters.

Calls for this resurrection of a racially homogeneous polity are beginning to be made explicit. Glenn Ellmers, writing on behalf of the MAGA-supporting, CRT-bashing Claremont Institute co-established by Hillsdale's Larry Arnn, insists that more than "half the country" – those supporting Biden and the Democrats – are not "authentic Americans." They are "hostile" to "America's ancient principles [of liberty and virtue] in prac- tice." The racial resonance to the message is delivered through abiding racist proxies: Those who are "a zombie or a human rodent" committed to a "shadow-life of timid conformity" should "go and memorize the poetry of Amanda Gorman" (the young Black poet who memorably read at Biden's Presidential inauguration). Ellmer's essay is a call, by contrast, to "[r]eal men and women who love honor and beauty" to prepare not merely for conservativism but for "counter-revolution" by "[l]earn[ing] some useful skills, stay[ing] healthy, and get[ting] strong" as "strong people are harder to kill." The "strong," implicitly, are presumed to be single-minded, like-looking, and same-thinking. To realize this outcome, "conservativism" indeed "is not enough."[29]

Senator Ted Cruz has grabbed this microphone at every opportunity, capitalizing on the success of Glen Youngkin's election to the Virginia governorship in November 2021.

Youngkin embraced the attacks on CRT. Appealing to "parental rights," he promoted parental disaffection with local school
boards supposedly supporting the teaching of CRT in schools.
Cruz quickly followed Youngkin's election with a public lecture for the Leadership Institute. The Institute turned it into an
eBook (albeit only ten pages long) which can be downloaded for
free, though requires providing an email address. What follows
are repeated email requests, which have a cult-recruitment feel
to them, to donate to the Leadership Institute. Donations are
used to promote campaigns, numbering 200-plus nationally,
to take over local school boards.

Cruz repeats Rufo's characterization of CRT rehearsed
above. His central projection is that CRT promotes "*anti-
white* racism."[30] Garrett Ziegler, a former White House aide
to Trump's economic advisor Peter Navarro, sought to dismiss the Congressional January 6 Committee investigating
the attack on the Capitol following Trump's loss in the 2020
Presidential election. The Committee, he declared running
together longstanding anti-communism with racial religios-
ity, consisted of "Bolsheviks" targeting "white Christians" like
him. This assertion of racial reversibility represents the super-
charging force of *deregulating racism*.

*

Trufist attacks on CRT are designed to undercut the traditional
understanding of racisms as targeting those deemed not white.
CRT was conceived originally as the analytic to identify and
promote the necessary conceptual understanding and conditions to constrain and end structural racism. Deregulating
racism allows for racism to be redirected as experienced by
whites exclusively. What it seeks to achieve by this is to strip
racism of its traditional charge while licensing whites to use
"any means necessary" to "defend themselves." This includes
two principal strategies.

First, proponents and practitioners of deregulating racism
want to divest civil rights laws of their legal force. Consider

the attacks on voting rights as a way of curtailing the votes of people of color. And second, they are concerned to dispossess the concept of racism of its critical force, entitling whites to say and do anything without constraint, notably mobilizing racist terms and targets. If racism as conventionally understood is not anymore racism, then racism can be promoted anew, with no recrimination. For example, conservatives, including Republican congressmen, were quick to launch racially charged attacks of inherent incompetence on the list of people President Biden was reported to be considering as his potential nominee for the first Black woman Justice on the Supreme Court, despite the eminent qualifications of those listed. The endpoint of this twofold strategy is white self-advancement posing as combating racism, presumptively against them.

Targeting CRT places this drive into gear. It takes aim at what constitutes "acceptable" historical memory of America's past as well as at the institutions of social mobility and advancement. Arch-conservatives, overwhelmingly white and male, are looking to hold onto power, politically and economically, by weaving together a series of tactics. Operationalizing the strategies of controlling school curricula and voter suppression, these tactics include: gerrymandered voting districts in Republican controlled states to ensure the artifice of Republican, and so white, electoral majorities; and renewed attacks on affirmative action, appealing to the Supreme Court's current majority to rule it unconstitutional. A right-wing group, 1776 Action, is working to make the "anti-American indoctrination" of race in education central to future elections.[31] And this requires also extensively controlling the narrative of historical memory, of what America "really" is and stands for, and who the state should serve.

The teaching of histories of slavery, Jim Crow racism, and the Civil Rights struggle in schools is being nationally targeted by Trufist-friendly groups. In European schools the teaching targets are nationally based colonial histories. This targeting seeks to write these themes out of Americans' and Europeans' respective self-understandings. It is to whitewash the story America or European nations tell (about) themselves. Trufism is nostalgia for an imagined idyll. It represents an order of things bleached of its blood stains, a past purified of its patterns of racially produced domination, segregation, and sustained inequity. Self-entitlement dies hard. Its defensive narrative cements into a non-negotiable wall of self-enclosure. The writing out of racism, the dual sense of racisms' underwriting, from American or European histories is the bedrock of deregulating racism.

Trufist erasure of CRT effectively undertakes to make difficult, if not impossible, the critical targeting of conventional racism. Racism can be read as nothing else but narrowly construed individual acts of wayward people, the worm wiggling its way through the otherwise perfect apple. The Trufer drive is to purge any possibility for people of color to talk in their own terms about themselves, their experiences and interests. The project is to delete all racially critical language. It is to obstruct the marginalized from defending themselves in the face of onslaughts in any way other than as individuals.

Josh Mandel ran as a Trumpist candidate in Ohio's Senate race. At a rally, he turned to the Trufist talking point to dismiss CRT. This included predictably invoking MLK's urging to treat people on the basis of their character, not skin color. King's daughter, Berenice, requested on social media that Mandel refrain from abusing her father's legacy to attack CRT. MLK, she wrote, "was not a drum major for colorblind society but for justice, which requires truth about our past and present." Mandel responded that Ms. King, and her brother Martin Luther King III who publicly concurred with his sister, had "no idea what [their] father preached." Calling Berenice King a "race profiteer," Mandel reiterated that "Critical Race Theory teaches kids to be racist" and "stomps on the grave of Martin Luther King."[32]

At the time of Ketanji Brown Jackson's Supreme Court nomination hearing, Indiana Republican Senator Mike Braun was making a case for reinvigorating state rights. Asked by a journalist if this commitment entailed that legislation regarding "interracial marriage" should be left to state determination rather than deemed federally unconstitutional as it was in 1968, the Senator affirmed that this should be left to state jurisdiction. (Like mine, Judge Jackson's marriage is interracial. Were Braun's suggestion realized, a marriage license for interracial couples in one state once more might not be recognized in another one. The very suggestion is insulting.) Deregulated racism entails that racial futures should mirror the pre-Civil Rights past.

These instances are deregulating racism put to practice. Deregulated racism frees up racial expression (speech, acts, practices). It opens the door to racial vilification, to licensing the killing, characterologically and actually, of those considered not white. Deregulating racism, it follows, is a form of racism that renders permissible a range of other pernicious acts.

MLK's aspiration notwithstanding, "character" has traditionally been racially judged, as racial ascriptions like "laziness," "conniving," "cunning," and "welfare queen," but also "honesty," rationality," and "hardworking" attest.[33] "Racial profiteering" can be added to this list, given its explicit invocation. Rufo has been prone to such judgments too. He has publicly mocked Kendi for changing his name and including "X." as a middle initial. In this, Rufo has shown complete insensitivity and failure, as I noted earlier, to appreciate the importance of self-naming in Black culture, given the history of erased and white ascribed names to Blacks in slavery and waged work.

Colorblindness, in the U.S., and racial erasure – non-racialism – in post-war Europe, are the articulations through which Trufer anti-anti-racism gets enacted. Racelessness is simply the refusal to use race as *terms* or explicit references. Being colorblind or nominally raceless, however, does not necessarily entail being *race*-refusing. If Trufers largely believe it wrong to use offensive terms, like the "n-word," then they must be race-conscious. Those who care less about the use obviously are too. As it is Black or Brown people about whom those professing racelessness are largely mindful, they are inevitably color-conscious. Racelessness in a deeply racially structured state, then, presupposes being race-aware. They are disposed to preserving white power, profitability, and purity.

In any case, if character is to be the basis of judgment, Trufers have surely failed the acid test. First, they have straightforwardly exhibited ignorant, insulting arrogance. There's a self-entitling insistence to "own" MLK's one line, while ignoring the rest of his critical analysis. Mandel especially makes explicitly racial charges, parading in terms of racelessness. That these are the outbursts Trufism is prompting with increasing abundance makes clear its commitment to a raceless racist politics, to deregulating racisms.

Trufism's "deregulating racism," accordingly, is as much a political strategy as an ideology. Perhaps ideologies always entail political strategies regarding pressing concerns, just as political strategies embed ideological presumption. The aim of Trufism has been to provide the tools for whitewashing race and racism, to render them the undiscussables of American politics, culture, and education. Undiscussable but expressible only for the purpose of shutting down critical rejoinders. It is a "redprint" for controlling by silencing any critical anti-racist narrative. The Free to Learn Coalition's "freedom from a singular worldview" is just that, the excising from possible discussion of a view made singular, that one they mark commonly with the moniker "CRT"!

Radical activists in Virginia Beach have sought to ban Toni Morrison's *The Bluest Eye* from the high-school curriculum in their school district. The undertaking to ban Morrison's work has had wider resonance in the state, and in other states like Missouri and Texas. From 2013 onwards, a Fairfax County, Virginia's mother has been trying to get Morrison's noted novel, *Beloved*, banned (Fairfax County is just across the river from Washington DC). *Beloved* is famously based on an actual historical account of a young enslaved mother killing her two-year-old daughter to protect her from slavery's horrors. The Virginia mother had complained that her son had nightmares from having had to read the novel for his high-school college preparation level courses (her son has gone on to become a lawyer with the National Republican Congressional Committee). She expressed "disgust" at the "bestiality" Morrison writes about, and was unable to read on herself after the first few pages. Her complaint featured prominently in the closing days of the 2021 Virginia Governor election race in an advertisement for Republican candidate Youngkin. He declared himself ready upon election to ban all CRT materials and teaching in state schools, and did so on his first day in office. Youngkin also rewarded the Heritage Foundation's influence in his anti-CRT campaign by appointing Angela Sailor as Virginia's "diversity officer." Sailor, a vocal critic of "CRT," served as Chief of Staff to Heritage President James.

In seeking parental control over school curricula, right-wing parents are trying to prevent almost college level teenagers being exposed to the history of bestiality and other horrors that writers like Morrison and Colson Whitehead in *The Underground Railroad* have so vividly conveyed as America's repressed memory of enslavement. In the year from March 2021, nearly 1,600 books focusing on Black or LGBTQ+ experiences have been challenged or prohibited in public libraries. Indeed, a movement has spawned nationally among conservatives, in part mobilized by Moms for Liberty, to close down public libraries because they serve as repositories for anti-racist and LGBTQ+ literature. Psychological repression requires keeping the memory trunk tightly locked. Deregulating racism makes possible the banning, and in some cases the burning, of books by Black authors revealing the history of racisms' horrors.

Colorblindness is a key feature of this politics in the U.S., both ideologically and strategically. Whites have seen themselves throughout American history in racially affirmative terms. That whiteness is now being characterized critically, whites want to refuse to be seen racially at all. Hence the stress on colorblindness. But, in insisting on colorblindness, radical whites want also to block Blacks from seeing themselves affirmatively qua Black (at least in terms whites don't control). Having been racially negated as Black historically, Trufers are refusing to see Blacks qua Black affirmatively by requiring that Black people not see themselves and not be seen as Black at all. They are seeing Blacks as Black so as not to see them, and not have them see themselves, as Black.

As it seems inevitable that American demography is a lost conservative battle, the self-declared Trufer war has shifted. Who controls the levers of power? And who controls dominant cultural representation, the racial story that the country over-ridingly rehearses to itself? There is a larger political revelation embedded in Mark Levin's and others' attacks on the supposition that CRT thinks of society as structured only in terms of oppressor and oppressed. This, perhaps inadvertently, makes clear that the radical right is out to accompany its attacks on democracy, rights, and government with an undertaking of erasure of core concepts such as "oppression." What conservative advocates are concerned to do, in the U.S. and more generally, is remove not just any critical language regarding race and racism. They are seeking to erase the very concepts along with the understandings they motivate that make clear how societies constitute themselves repeatedly through orderings of (racially) oppressed and oppressing subject positions. That the definition of these concepts is left nebulous and open-ended enables their ready and repeated mobilization as easy targets for dismissal across the field of the political.

Nikole Hannah-Jones is the investigative journalist who spearheaded the *New York Times* 1619 Project, which aimed to retell the history of the U.S. through slavery and its legacies. The fight over historical memory, as she has aptly characterized the attacks on the 1619 Project, is not just about how to understand the American past. Through understanding that past, the defining version of our contemporary condition is being contested too. Trufism undertakes to re-establish the grounds for who more-or-less fully belongs (one can make similar arguments about the policing of membership in European countries where "CRT," "decolonization," or "postcoloniality" are under attack too). It seeks to express the narrowed counter-terms and conditions for social belonging (whether as American or European), for acceptable and unacceptable thought, in our time.

Trufism purges the histories of racism, refusing to address the structuring that race has etched deep into the social fabric. In doing so, it seeks to re-inscribe inherited legacies of race and racism as indelible, because invisible, features of the country's landscape. The emphasis on colorblindness without redressing the inherited impacts of structural and systemic racisms just reiterates what critical race analysts like Eduardo Bonilla-Silva, Crenshaw, and others have been calling out as "raceless racisms" for the past twenty-five years. It has set in place the inherited order of social standing absent the unjust conditions making that sustained hierarchy possible.

In appealing loudly to "living free," Trufist ideologues are licensing themselves free to do away with all opposition. By mobilizing to cancel CRT, to regulate it, they are working to silence any resistance to their undertaking to install minority rule. Mitch McConnell revealingly declared that "African American voters are voting in just as high a percentage as Americans," implying that the former are not really or fully

American. Resonances of the three-fifths clause, not to mention fraudit. The undertaking *to deregulate* extends the structural conditions that enable a demographic, political, and electoral minority to continue ruling over the rest. They are doing so, in part, by removing the very language by which to identify racial oppressor over oppressed, past and forward-looking.

Texas is leading the way. Over the past decade, 95 percent of the state's population increase has been among people not identified as white, especially Hispanics. Texas Hispanics today number more-or-less equally to whites. In re-districting for the next decade, Texas has increased majority white voting districts by two, to twenty-three, reducing Hispanic majority districts by one to seven, and Black majority districts to zero.[34] Contestable voting districts, those where there is no clear electoral majority for either major party, have been reduced from eleven, to none.

Inspired by Texas, Florida's Governor DeSantis is challenging the key anti-discrimination provision of the 1964 Voting Rights Act designed to protect the vote for those historically disenfranchised by race. His state electoral map reduces majority African-American voting districts previously represented by Democrats from four to now two. This would ensure Republicans, tending overwhelmingly to be represented by white legislators, control 20 of 28 Congressional seats, in a state whose voters are quite evenly divided between Republicans and Democrats.

*

The Trufer surge to deregulate racism is meant to help pave the way for structuring and rationalizing the conditions to support white minority rule for the foreseeable future. Mary Miller, a Republican Congresswoman for Illinois, declared that the overturning of a constitutional right to abortion by the U.S. Supreme Court in June 2022 was "a victory for *white* life." She tried rationalizing away the claim as meaning to say "a victory for the right to life." But there is a logic, if pernicious, to her abortion claim. States itching to ban abortion following the Supreme Court ruling are those dominated by conservative legislatures with shrinking white majority populations they would like to preserve as the country more broadly diversifies. Race is barely a subtext here.

The neoliberal deregulation of economic activity taking hold from the 1980s on was invariably paired with a more socially restrictive state. Neoliberalism famously stressed individual freedom and curtailment of social and state constraint and regulation of economic activity. It complements this individualizing of responsibility with erasure of any historical and so structural account of how present social conditions are produced out of past structures. The funding and militarization of policing steadily escalated from that period too, accompanied by an intensification of the racial criminalization of social life, most notably the war on drugs, dramatic prison expansion, and the attendant increase in racially indexed incarceration. The deregulation of racism being exercised today extends this logic. The freeing up of racist expression broadly underway has been achieved through restrictive legislation targeting CRT and pretty much all anti-racist activism and critique. It is paired with conservative calls for increased policing budgets and unrestricted policing tactics. Barack Hussein Obama's election in 2008 was less "the end of white America"[35] than a signal to strident conservatives of the need for its make-over.

Philosophers have distinguished between negative and positive liberty.[36] Conservativism's commitment conventionally has been to negative liberty, freedom *from* state imposition. Positive freedom – the claim *to* state provision of baseline social resources for citizens – has been assumed protected by rights (what conservatives, with increasing stridency as neoliberalism took hold, dismiss as state-protected or welfare entitlements). Deregulating racism upends this convention.

In a novel turn, Trufers are seeking to entangle negative liberty with positive freedom. They are demanding liberty *from* state limits on their expression in order to say and do whatever advances their self-entitling power, increasingly as they face impending minority status demographically and politically. Racial neoliberalism[37] pairs deregulating racism (liberty *from* state oversight and limitation on racist expression) with delimiting anti-racist and social diversification initiatives (freedom *to* restrict any expression critical of racism or any effort further diluting white numbers). For example, a national group, "Moms for *Liberty*" (my emphasis), seeks to police what *all* children can read, working to ban anti-racist and LGBTQ+ books from school and public libraries. So, Trufers entitle themselves to engage in whatever racist or anti-non-gender-binary expression they please, while silencing all critical rejections of such expression. Think of this as exemplifying what political theorist Elizabeth Anker has usefully called "ugly freedoms."[38] Ugly freedoms are not just the freedoms to do ugly things. They represent the contortion of thinking to establish the doing of those ugly acts as an inviolable right.

This self-entitlement, in turn, is made possible by two waves of the wand. First, conventional racisms are declared over, frozen in the past, simply historical relics.[39] This, too, is enabled by neoliberal thinking. Neoliberalism stressed its condition as "the end of history," a delinking or break from the past, refusing to see the past as having produced or even enabled the de-historicized present. This clears the way for the fabricating of the past, in the ways we have seen Trufism licensing itself to do. Structural and systemic racism are a thing of the past, Trufers insist. Individuals are solely responsible for their racist (speech) acts.

Second, and relatedly, the deregulating of racism is hidden behind the veil of colorblind racelessness. If race is unseen, racism – that is, discrimination by appealing to race – can be pronounced a figment. Deregulating racism liberates racisms by rendering them nameless, effectively invisible, or at least unpronounceable, in plain sight.

Historically conventional racisms were about establishing, maintaining, and extending control of the state. Such racisms were largely bald and explicit because racial discourse was the vernacular, as much the grammar of science, literature, religious life, and high culture as of the street and the everyday. It was the language in and through which power expressed itself.

Deregulating racism is the contemporary form racism is increasingly assuming. Race is being erased, racism conventionally forbidden if far from unpracticed. Deregulating racism represents the reinvention of a racism for white slippage if not quite from power, then for loss of control, lest it slide completely from grasp. In seeking to give a veneer of colorblind – of raceless – respectability to white power, deregulating racism couldn't but help unchaining while remaking White Power too. Deregulating racism, additionally, is a racism that deregulates, licensing violence against African Americans, Asians, and Latinos, or at least neither seeking to restrict nor condemn such acts or their threats.

One further feature underscores the ways neoliberalism enables deregulating racism. Neoliberal thinking stresses short-term, individually produced economic profit, while ignoring more extended consequences (for example, the social implications of deeply regressive tax cuts, soaring personal and social debt, mortgage swaps and derivatives, etc.). Trufism operates on the same logic, politically applied. The reach is for immediate personal or political victory, no matter the dire individual or social longer-term consequences.

Restoration projects always look to re-make, the new assuming the veneer of the replaced while updating its product for the contemporary eye and ear. Deregulating racism is racism's restoration project for our times.

10

Executing Critical Race Theory

Rufo and his followers reduce any substantive criticism of racism to a distant semblance of Critical Race Theory. CRT is identified almost exclusively with the least compelling CRS statements, often decontextualized, by the likes of Kendi and DiAngelo. Structural and systemic racism are scoffed at, in favor of reducing conventional racism overwhelmingly to exceptional *individual* wrongdoing. Rufo and the politicians he fuels have said next to nothing acknowledging the slew of murders of Black, Brown, and Asian people, preferring to vilify school districts who use "tragedy to promote hate" by teaching children about racism.

Extending neo-conservative formulation from the 1980s on, Trufism diminishes, obscures, or denies histories of racially driven degradation. Any critical focus on structure is censored, personal agency elevated. The experiences of police brutality and institutional racism are ignored, or swatted away. Conventional racisms are deregulated, and so licensed. Trufers generally follow the dictum of seventeenth-century philosopher Thomas Hobbes: whatever is not explicitly curtailed by law is permitted. Almost all criticisms of racism Trufers work to proscribe. Threats of violence against Black people and institutions have dramatically surged, as made evident by the ongoing bomb threats to dozens of Historically Black Colleges and Universities (HBCUs) from late January 2022, about which political critics of CRT have had nothing to say. CRT is misleadingly reduced in origin or elaboration exclusively to Marxism. And every "critical race theorist" is made to sound like the cardboard cutout of Kendi. This is not critique, or even criticism. It is dangerous caricature.

The inexactness and imprecision in the Trufist account of what CRT amounts to is key to the political initiative. The vagueness makes it easier for conservative lawmakers and activists everywhere to target CRT because their supporters are demanding it. A form of political marketization, Trufism delivers to consumers the demands it has mostly shaped for them. Trufism is like the algorithm that has consumers "choosing" the product it has prompted them to order. Close to anything can be made to count as "racially" conceived, as Trufers have discovered. Once targeted, it can be summarily censored, excised, canceled.

Christopher Rufo's current employer, the Manhattan Institute, has fashioned model anti-CRT legislation to advocate for state legislatures to adopt. Rufo ends his Briefing Book with similar materials. These include standard language exhorting politicians to legislate against adopting or teaching CRT in state institutions alongside language for state legislation. Other activist organizations such as the Citizens for Renewing America and the Heritage Foundation are promoting such stylized dictates too. While racisms are being freed up, restrictions on anti-racisms and criticisms of racism, including teaching racisms' histories, are proliferating. School diversity initiatives are being cut back or completely curtailed as a consequence.

In undertaking to remove or radically reduce the terms of race for identifying discrimination, there is a deeper logic being advanced. The Heritage strategy of straitjacketing CRT in order to attack and diminish its impact is paired with the push to discourage voting, especially for urban and younger voters of color. In the 2022 mid-term primary elections, Texas rejected 13 percent of mail-in ballots as ineligible (up from two percent in 2018) as a result of newly introduced restrictions. The wiping out of critical tools to identify and respond to racism makes it harder to uncover voter suppression, resulting in disparate racial impact. This erasure renders it next to impossible to mark such disparate racial outcomes as racist.

As I indicated at the outset, politicians and intellectual influencers in Britain and continental Europe have mimicked the terms of Trufism as applied to their own political contexts. The objects of their attacks differ, given the political and historical differences in each nation-state. In Europe generally, the legacy of colonialism looms larger in political concern than in the U.S. So, in France and Germany the mainstream political pushback has been against "postcolonialism" and "decolonialization." A far-right candidate in the run-up to the French presidential election invoked Renaud Camus's "great replacement" slogan to appeal to right-supporting voters venting about immigration. In Britain, the local economic legacies of plantation slavery have been denied, debates around the profiteering connection of country houses to slave plantation financing have been parodied, and questioning the propriety of monumentalizing slavers and colonizers has been summarily dismissed. European leaders and their intellectual supporters may resist "importing American academicisms." Yet, in supposedly resisting "cancel culture," they have been the ones pushing its practice, doing so in the terms of the very Americanisms they claim to reject.

*

Critical Race Theory as both a legal and more broadly social analytic dates to the late 1970s and 1980s. Trufism was foisted on the U.S. from September 2020. When all is said and done, and the hurling of trumped-up charges fade across time, one must step back and ask how convincing Trufist accounts are. From 1980 to 2020, the U.S. lived through twenty-four years of Republican presidencies. How plausible is it, then, that prior to the Trufer self-pronouncement in the waning moments of the Trump period, no parent across America had volubly complained that their white children were all being told they were bad because white while all the little Black kids were getting glowing affirmation that they were good because Black? American linguist John McWhorter expressly dates the emergence of "woke racism" in America's public schools to June 2020, in the wake of the urban street protests that rocked the country.[1] It is worth noting that students were on summer vacation then. "Wokeness" has substituted for "political correctness," popular on the right a half-decade ago, surfacing the racial significance operating of late. Tom Klingenstein, chair of the Claremont Institute's board and its principal donor, has taken to declaring all of America's current ailments to "woke communism" (memically foreshortened to "wokecom").[2]

Trufers offer decontextualized anecdotes as examples, not any data. McWhorter's characterization of "woke racism" similarly provides no empirical account of the "phenomenon." The Trufer version of CRT is make-believe. McWhorter's tone seemingly more measured and even-handed, his examples of institutional "woke racism" reveal their own reductionism. He draws the title of his late 2021 book from Rufo's Briefing Book (2020) and the popular social media derision that followed regarding the term. As an instance of "woke racism," he cites the California Department of Education's "Mathematics Framework":

> Empowering students with mathematics also includes removing the high stakes of errors and sending the message that learning is always unfinished and that it is safe to take mathematical risks. This mind-set creates the conditions for students to develop a sense of ownership over their mathematical thinking and their right to belong to the discipline of mathematics.[3]

McWhorter glosses this as "a truly artful way of saying that 'diverse' kids should not be saddled with the onerous task of having to get the actual answers," what he calls "Critical Race Theory Lite."[4] Really? Can the state not be read as trying to open spaces for students of all stripes and backgrounds, from those whose homes are less able to support their learning to those with significant learning challenges and lack of technological access, not least faced with difficulties exacerbated by the pandemic, to learn mathematics, at their own pace? The state is recognizing that standardized learning negatively impacts children of many backgrounds (it is McWhorter, ironically, who is reading "diversity" racially insinuated into the quoted statement).

Mathematics obviously has right and wrong answers. Yet there can be different ways of arriving at correct outcomes, often with cultural assumptions embedded in them. That these assumptions can disadvantage some in their learning is reason to be open to diverse learning paths.[5] Instead of burying some children's interest in a technical subject beneath dismissal, California's statement might better be read as seeking a variety of ways to support igniting a passion. Can that actually be faulted? Is it not better than Florida's banning of 28 school mathematics texts because they incorporated very occasional workbook examples addressing racial disparities in sickle cell anemia or implicit bias? Most of Florida's censored math books were cut because they used social-emotive learning. Rufo has rejected social-emotional learning (SEL), with no evidence, as "a delivery mechanism for radical pedagogies such as critical race theory and gender deconstructionism" in order to "rewire their behavior according to the dictates of left-wing ideology." (Florida cut one textbook because a page encouraged collaborative learning rather than stressing individual responsibility.) Twenty-five states have introduced restrictions on SEL for being a subterfuge for promoting CRT. Trufism's abiding concern is not with learning but with erasure of any critical terms and tools that might contest their own racial and gendered domination.

The relatively small handful of embarrassing CRT examples identified by Trufers in schools or teaching materials is repeated by their followers ad nauseam. These often (are meant to) bury the more compelling insights about how racisms undermine learning. Examples, no matter how embarrassing and accurate, tagged with labels like "wokeism," however, do not amount to a theory, or even analysis. Perhaps the source any time such claims are circulated should give pause about their accuracy, and especially about the feasibility of the interpretation ascribed to the cited events and expressions. Rufo and his colorblind crowd have evidenced repeatedly that any example of CRT excess advanced by them requires heightened scrutiny for its plausibility, context, and representativeness.

The charge of this or that being CRT – a superintendent, principal, or teacher effectively being the agitating commie in the corridor or classroom – would be laughable if their lives and livelihoods weren't so readily placed at risk. James Whitfield was the first Black high-school principal appointed in the Texan town of Colleyville. The day after George Floyd was killed in May 2020, Dr. Whitfield published a heartfelt, non-accusatory letter to the school community. He called for public recognition of systemic racism and working together to be rid of it. The community response was overwhelmingly supportive. Once CRT assumed its Trufist ring in October 2020, a local resident called out the popular principal in the almost all-white town for practicing, what else, "Critical Race Theory." Holiday photographs of Whitfield embracing his bikini-clad white wife on a beach ten years earlier were dug up from the depths of his Facebook account. The hint of interracial sexuality between an attractive couple surfaced barely suppressed anxieties. Whitfield was eventually suspended on paid leave. He was then denied renewal of his school contract by an all but completely white school board, despite widespread vocal community support for his reinstatement.[6] A board member affiliated with Patriot Mobile, mentioned in the previous chapter, played an instrumental role in his removal. She referred to Whitfield as "a total activist" for writing the community letter that got him fired.

Trufer "victory" in cases like this comes at the price of a promising career. It is also at the cost to an education preparing youth to think for themselves while negotiating an increasingly heterogeneous world. That's the larger loss from deregulating racisms, likewise difficult to recuperate once erased.

There are obvious reasons that right-wing politicians and academics, much like conservative media outlets, so readily take their lead on CRT from Rufo and his partners. Political convenience and the popularity of Trufism are two. Willful misunderstanding and misinterpretation of what CRT in fact stands for is matched only by intentional ignorance of the enduring impacts of structural and personal racisms.

Rufo declares CRT "the new orthodoxy" in public institutions such as schools, universities, government agencies, even the military in America. At least seventy bills restricting the teaching of CRT and critical gender issues are working themselves through state legislatures, a number of which have been passed to date. Texas Lt. Governor Dan Patrick has proposed firing faculty at Texas public universities for teaching some undefined version of CRT. Tennessee lawmakers are following suit. The Leadership Institute has unveiled "CampusReform," a website "to monitor" and "expose" the "left-wing agenda on college campuses." Resonances of McCarthyism are too obvious to pass by without noting. Actually, it is Trufism, Rufo's "CRT," that has become the new activist orthodoxy of contemporary conservativism, in major media outlets like Fox, at school-board meetings, in Republican-controlled state legislatures. At schools, or on their websites, you may find the occasional awkward assertion about "Diversity, Equity, Inclusion" (DEI). But you'll be hard pressed to turn up anything compellingly representative of CRT anywhere in schools. Trufism is to schooling what fraudit is to voting: a political "fix" in search of manufacturing a social problem.

Are there K-12 classes actually teaching anything like "racial essentialism," "interest convergence," and "intersectionality"? Or that "all whites are the oppressors" and "all Blacks the oppressed"? Khiara Bridges, a law professor at the University of California, Berkeley, and author of an impressive CRT textbook,[7] has pointed out that nobody would claim that legal doctrines like Law and Economics or Feminist Law, readily taught in electives at law schools, are on offer at K-12 schools. How is it that CRT is deemed so simple or enticing that kids can be brainwashed to believe it? Once again, lawyers of color, Black legal scholars, and academics are being reduced to child-ish thought. If Harvard Law-trained Senators and Governors can't explain precisely what CRT in fact is (they could avoid those electives), would most teenagers really pass this test? And if they can, perhaps their efforts should be applauded rather than castigated.

For Trufism, CRT is simply code for *any* expression critical of racism, as I have said. It is a way to dismiss all criticisms of racism without having to take them seriously or make any effective arguments about them. One has to say, though: if you have to fake the doctrine to criticize or reject it, this hints at anxiety about what the real thing is revealing.

*

America, @realchrisrufo has told us, "remains the most tolerant, welcoming, and diverse society in history."[8] Such assertions inevitably cover up deeper insecurities. The histori-cal record is invariably mixed. The country's history bears this out: decimation and isolation of the indigenous; slavery, freed Blacks under Jim Crow and beyond; the Chinese Exclusion Act, Japanese internment. But also suspicion upon their initial arrival toward anyone presumed not white and Protestant: Jews, Irish, Italians. The first Catholic President, in 1960, was hardly universally welcomed, and not just because of political disagreement (though all six Republican-appointed Supreme Court Justices currently are Catholic). The first Black President wasn't until 2008, the first Black and woman Vice-President sworn in only in 2021. There have been no Jewish, Italian, or Latino Presidents or Vice-Presidents, for all of it. Native Americans, local inhabitants a touch longer than the rest of us combined (who exactly was welcoming whom?), celebrated their first cabinet Secretary appointment, in 2021. To date, the only EU country (including Britain before Brexit) led by any person of color has been Ireland.

Perhaps Rufo might ask the families of those murdered by vigilantes and white supremacists or wrongfully killed by police whether they would concur with his assessment. Trufism's mantric lauding of America's unstinting greatness represents, against the backdrop I list here, one version of what the late Lauren Berlant famously analyzed as "cruel optimism," the inevitable dashing of raised hope.[9] America's "greatness" is often celebrated. Racial arrangement is not what it was pre-1964, to be sure. One might ask, nevertheless, whether the supposed greatness would not be better enhanced by comprehending the complexities of its variegated history than by burying them alive.

The capacity of racisms to metamorphose and reinvent suggests that the more compelling metaphor for facing them down is less a race or war to be won than a morphing viral condition to be effectively managed and curtailed. Just as many are baulking at constraints to control a viral pandemic, so too with regulating racisms.

It is important to stress that a key modern social principle is equality for all. This is an aspirational goal for which we continue to strive and struggle, as both the Reconstruction Amendments and the Civil Rights Act remind us. The importance is in the framing principles, the possibility to reach for their universal implementation even, and especially, in the face of the invariable resistances accompanying this history to this day. Legal advances can be undone, as the 2013 Supreme Court erasure of the 1965 Voting Rights Act pre-clearance clause attests. Both the founding principles and the constant aspirational struggles and strategies for their full(er) implementation, along with the violent pushbacks against them, need to be taught. That is the point of both CRT and CRS, properly understood, notwithstanding their sometimes slippages.

A baseline of common historical knowledge is key both to collective social co-existence and a capacity to resist revisionist erasure. In a September 2022 address, Governor DeSantis declared that

> the American revolution . . . caused people to question slavery. Nobody had questioned it before we decided as Americans that we are endowed by our creator with inalienable rights and that we are all created equal. Then that birthed abolition movements.

Claims to American exceptionalism invariably mangle the historical record. Slaves in the American colonies didn't need the American Revolution to know that slavery was inherently wrong. Slave revolts manifested at least as early as 1700. There were legislative and civic debates in Spain about slavery's impropriety through much of the sixteenth century. The first French abolition was effected by Louis V, in 1315. The second, in 1794, was prompted less by the American example than by the Haitian Revolution (1791) and France's own Rights of Man (1789). It took a Civil War some seven decades later for American abolition (1863) to follow suit. Florida, notably, belonged to the Confederacy.

Rufo's performative celebration of America's greatness ends his late 2021 hit piece in *City Journal*. The article adds an exclamation point to my line of argument. Rufo reports receiving "a trove" of leaked "whistleblower documents" about Google's

(Alphabet's) "re-education program." Quotes from the leaked materials are liberally splashed throughout the article, with no references and so no way of checking them. Rufo's targets, once more, are declarations of America as "a system of white supremacy" and its population "raised to be racist." Kendi and Hannah-Jones again are the fall guys, their respective talks for Google employees taken by the article as if both CRT and Google statements. The same can be said of an internal reading list created by employees explicitly deemed by Google to be "unofficial."

Within two days of Rufo's publication about Google, all the major right-wing outlets had reported his "findings," virtually verbatim. These included Fox News, of course, *Washington Examiner*, the *New York Post*, *The Federalist*, *National Review*, and Murdoch's *Daily News* in London. The great Google was being brought to its knees by the fearless crusader. There seemed not the least effort by any of these publications to confirm Rufo's claims independently. Indignation sells.

Rufo provides no context for Google's efforts to soften its image. The company has a history of not hiring many Black employees, even less so at managerial levels. Black and Brown workers at Google had complained repeatedly of "disrespect" and "dehumanization." In December 2020, a very public dispute surfaced some of the discontent. Timnit Gebru is a notable artificial intelligence researcher of Ethiopian family background, then with the leading Google Brain initiative. She expressed criticism in a co-authored conference paper of Google's work on machine learning. The criticisms were directed pointedly at Google's facial recognition failures regarding Blacks and women. She had likewise taken aim at Google's failed diversity hiring practices. To cut a complicated story short, Gebru's employment terminated when she refused to submit to unreasonable censorship of her work and criticisms.[10]

The very public fallout from the firing moved Google to renew its efforts to diversify its global workforce.[11] The materials and efforts cited by Rufo appear to be connected to the company's mixed attempts to create a more open discussion about racism, Google's workplace conditions, structure, and climate. It didn't help that Alphabet had also just invited the Heritage Foundation President, Kay Coles James, to join their AI Ethics Committee to appease criticisms of one-sidedness they were receiving from conservatives. The materials and initiatives Rufo references suggest that Google has not been especially imaginative about those efforts. The company seems driven by some of its loudest critics rather than to think creatively about transforming workplace culture to be more respectful, inclusive, and sensitive. They have tended to follow the very conventional, mostly lip service initiatives on offer from standard DEI offerings.

Well into their efforts, in September 2021, a Black employee riding a bike across the Google campus, as many employees do, was stopped by security. Skeptical of his employee's ID, they proceeded to escort him off-campus (an old Black friend used to recount to me identical stories about the Stanford campus while a visiting faculty member there in the mid-1990s; he refused overtures to join the permanent faculty because of the experience). In all of this, Google exemplifies the challenges confronting the realm of technology more generally. Rufo has been stone-cold silent about any of this.

Google's efforts are not univocal. A leading European analyst of everyday racism, diversity, and gender issues was approached by a committee representing Google's European, Middle Eastern, and North African operations to talk to employees from the region. A skeptic about conventional corporate diversity efforts, she pressed for an open conversation with the committee both to get on the table what concerns exist at ground level and to think creatively in common about what responses and cultural change might amount to. Virtual attendees numbered in the many hundreds, the conversation frank and searching. Trufist reductionism serves no one but the ideologues. The question remains where Google ends up taking this. Trufism clearly will be of no help here.

Rufo, as we have seen, hardly has a reliable record of accuracy, whether in reporting or interpretation. I enjoyed a graduate school mentor who urged his students to find the interpretation of material we were reading most likely to make the material appear true. That interpretation, he suggested somewhat generously, would be the compelling one. The Trufist method is exactly the obverse. Find the interpretation of those with whom you disagree, those you want to make sound silly, that would sound least true, and broadcast it as loudly as possible so as to embarrass and ultimately bury it. That the "news" outlets simply hit repeat makes them not journalists but an ideological echo chamber. They are serving as the loudspeaker of the Big Racial Lie. St. George's Dragon was always mythical.

Trufers, then, have leveled fabricated charges at CRT. They have mercilessly tracked and pursued "it" behind a shield of these false charges. They have unleashed the national mob on it, hoisted it on the proverbial gallows, undertaking to strangle it. It is not too strong to call this a racially driven undertaking of public mob execution. Trufism is out to produce conceptual strange fruit hanging from the populist tree. Postcards of "proof" circulate on social media in the wake.

*

Trufer attacks on "Critical Race Theory," I have argued, represent the pernicious racial politics of Trumpism. The coordinated attacks are predicated on a more-or-less complete fabrication about CRT and the country's racial record. They presume denial of the persistence of structural racism, and of the debilitating impacts of the contemporary recourse to colorblindness. The Trufer undertaking, as I have demonstrated, is to recast racism as directed almost exclusively against whites while deregulating conventional racisms to run rampant. The driving point of all this is to extend white minority rule politically, legally, economically, and culturally in the face of impending white minoritarian demographic status.

Rufo's Twitter feed suggests he deeply believes his fabrication. As do his followers, mostly (some politicians peddling the nonsense are just plain cynical). It is less that Rufo is convincing than that the bill of sale on offer is all about race. Race enrages above all else. It blurs vision. That it was originally conceived as a doctrine of division has transposed to the charge that any attempt to counter it is divisive too. The anger it fuels endures in waves even as the bill of goods prompting the anger shifts. Abidingly self-serving and ideological, all the way down.

The Trufist targeting of CRT, however, signals a more extreme register in the supposed war against the war on racism. It is not that any invocation of race has not in the past been designated as (toying with or bordering on) racism. This, after all, has been the standard position in post-war Europe. What is new here, however, is that the Rufo bandwagon is pushing the point to a more heightened expression. The stress on colorblindness means that they exonerate themselves from being racist because not race-invoking.

Southern Baptists, the largest Protestant denomination in the U.S., home to many evangelicals, and mostly significant Trump supporters, have been wringing their hands over how to address CRT, the latest turn in their longstanding response to charges of racism. The concern loomed so large it became a major topic of discussion at their 2021 Convention. A leader had declared that "the Bible demands all Christians be colorblind." Of course, no literal claim like this exists in the New (or Old) Testament.

In response, John Dyer, a Dallas Seminary theologian, created a "colorblind" translation of the New Testament, the "Anti-Critical Race Theory (A.C.T.) Bible," on the projected premise that "Critical Theory, especially Critical Race Theory, is a major threat to Christianity's success." A.C.T. proposed replacing any terms in the Book to ensure readers are able to avoid "any characteristics that might lead one to have Marxist thoughts." Terms like "nation" were replaced by "something," "peoples" by "everyone," "balance, weights, scales, and measures" by "actions," "interactions," or "treatment." Any designation characterizing social position, office, or comparison was replaced with "person." The effect was to reduce all indirect referencing of groups and social justice – "centurion, Samaritan woman, Niger" – to individuation devoid of social positioning.

Within a month of publishing the website, Dyer admitted his translation was satirical. He had set out to show that the supposed obscenity of "Marxism" parading as "anti-racism" along with its colorblinding response would serve radically to alter both the meaning of Scripture and the histories embedded. He had made heads turn. At least someone has retained a critical sense of humor.[12]

In contrast to Dyer, the race-invoking are racist, for Trufism, by virtue simply of invoking racial distinction. Rufo's clan self-supposes that they cannot be racist because they have scrubbed their language of race, though as we have seen only by half. Critical race theorists, and anti-racists generally, *must* be "racist" simply by being, well, *race* theorists and activists. We are "racist" by invoking race to address racisms and their legacies. Racism, on this projection, is not about sustained separation, inequality, segregation, violence. It is reduced from material circumstance, now rendered less visible rather than redressed, simply to the language of (self-)characterization. It wasn't so far back that Black children were being told they had to work twice as hard to have an equal chance of getting ahead. So, if they can't keep up no matter how great their effort, they are now being admonished that this is solely their failing, their responsibility.

In the 1980s and 1990s the canon wars consumed higher education much as the attacks on CRT are doing with schools of late. What constituted college "must-read" literature to be considered a well-educated adult was overwhelmingly produced by white, European men. Augustine's *Confessions* was often on that list. Born to Berber parents in what is modern-day Algeria, Augustine studied in Carthage and ultimately returned from professional pursuits in Rome and Milan to spend his later life as Bishop of Hippo. Post-medieval European paintings represented him as white, even though he was in fact North African. The dominance of white male faculty across higher education effectively sought to reproduce a canon of literature in which they recognized themselves and which they ordained with greatness. The homogeneity of the canon came under acute contestation especially in the 1990s, as multiculturalism took hold. The college canon was opened up somewhat as a consequence, leading to more authors of diverse backgrounds being added, essentially as supplements.

This more diverse canon is under attack, most notably in the K-12 arena. Multiculturalism had a profound impact on school education too, varying the curriculum and the library, adding a wider range of literature and experience. Schools were beginning to reflect the country's gathering demographic heterogeneity. The attacks on CRT accordingly represent a quite radical undertaking to retrench and roll back this greater openness and diversification of the school canon. Making or keeping the canon "white" again is another constitutive feature of deregulating racism. Myopic white parents and lawmakers in states like Virginia, Tennessee, Florida, and Texas are mobilizing to ban from not just the classroom but the school and public libraries also any literature and histories not representative of their own experience, family heritage, and official historical narrative of the nation.

A state legislator in Texas sent a list of 850 book titles to all school districts across the state inquiring whether the books are taught or in school libraries, and how much was spent on acquiring them. The premise of the list is that the books "could make students feel uneasy." He clearly had aides compose the list on the basis of googling keywords on race and sex. Given the sprawling, sometimes obscure contents, I doubt the lawmaker or his aides had read all or any of the listed books. The legislator was a candidate for Texas Attorney General, looking (unsuccessfully, as it turned out) to raise his profile in a crowded primary field. Attacking stand-ins for CRT will apparently do that. The most recognizable names on the booklist included Kendi, of course, but also Ruby Bridges, Ta-Nehisi Coates, and Isabel Wilkerson. Notable authors included Margaret Atwood and Claudine Rankine, and academics Henry Louis Gates, Michelle Alexander, Nell Painter, Sara Ahmed, and Ilan Stavans. Perhaps most surprising was the inclusion of two national politicians, U.S. Senator Amy Klobuchar's autobiography, and Representative Jamie Raskin (the lead prosecutor on President Trump's second impeachment) for his book on, of all things, the Supreme Court for law students.[13] Student uneasiness, apparently, is produced by any political view not agreeing with a white parent's or legislator's.

Canonical literature operates on three related registers. First, it sets the standard for what the society takes to be excellent literature, both in form and in insightful or revelatory content: about the human condition and social structure, relation, and interaction. Second, it establishes the example of good and bad behavior, acceptable and unacceptable social engagement – for the country, and perhaps for all and all time. And third, it reinforces who is taken to belong or not, to be socially visible or unseen, who has no standing or even does not socially exist.

Works targeted for school and public library banning in the attacks on CRT include greats like Toni Morrison and James Baldwin. But there have been attempts also to excise more critical histories of slavery (the 1619 Project, but not only), stories about the experience of young Black children integrating urban schools in the 1960s under extraordinary duress, and accounts of LGBTQ+ experiences growing up. It is not that these protesting parents don't want just their own children "exposed" to such literature in the classroom. They don't want *any* children to be "polluted" in their thinking, lest it be passed on to theirs, and so libraries need to be "cleansed" too. School choice forever, but only for them.

In this, the anti-CRT protestors are like the extreme anti-vaxxers and anti-maskers. They are each fighting to be rid of the targeted culprit. And, imperiously, in taking to rid their own lives of it, they deem it necessary to rid it for all. The "official" canonical account of American life, past, present, and future, they are demanding, is that of, by, for, and reinforcing white America. Consider the revisionist DeSantis's claim about slavery abolition outlined above. CRT, in the elastic understanding Trufers have invested in it, contests all, from the defining standards to the content of the canon, and perhaps canonicity as such. The Rufo-inspired crowd accordingly find it imperative to shut it up, if not close it down.

Some parents in North Carolina objected to a school teacher showing twelve-year-olds an image of Kara Walker's silhouette artwork, *Gone*, because of its "sexually explicit" nature. As with Walker's work generally, *Gone* addresses violence against Black women, often of a suggestively sexual nature such as slave rape. A purposeful commentary on *Gone with the Wind*, this piece is more sexually suggestive than explicit. It is far less explicit than much of what kids can see or be shown by peers on their smartphones, though perhaps more evocative as a consequence. The very point of good art, after all. Would these parents have objected had the work viewed been Manet's *Bathers in the Forest* or Picasso's *Girl on the Ball*?

The attacks on CRT in schools are central to a larger, newly disturbing set of developments in American politics. Individuals, including children in schools, are being legally licensed to police and report on others. Agency is being elevated to trump structure, at every turn. The Texas abortion law has notoriously inscribed this into anti-abortion operation, fiscally rewarding those reporting violators of the law who have abortions or assist women to acquire them. Less reported is the fact that in states like Idaho school children are being encouraged to report teachers they determine are teaching some unarticulated version of "CRT."

Florida's Governor DeSantis introduced the "Stop the Woke (Wrongs to Our Kids and Employees) Act," modeled on the abortion law in Texas. Rufo, a resident of Washington State literally at the opposite end of the U.S. map, stood at the Governor's side at the public announcement. The legislation was subsequently passed by Florida's legislature. It licenses parents with "the private right" to sue if they consider their children are being taught CRT, in any version they project, or employees if they feel they are being subjected to CRT equity training in the workplace. Both could collect attorneys' fees and damages should they win. Companies can be sued for offering training suggesting that "virtues" like "merit" or "racial colorblindness" are racist.[14] In August 2022, Michael James, a veteran Florida primary school teacher preparing for a largely Black class of autistic children, placed images of exceptional Black leaders – MLK, Harriet Tubman, Colin Powell, and President Obama – on the class notice board and table. A school district "behavior analyst" sent to help him set up his classroom removed the images, telling him they were "student inappropriate." She was apparently expressing her personal judgment, not following orders. James resigned in protest.

Tennessee has introduced legislation for college students similar to laws in Texas and Florida. Mississippi's outlawing of teaching CRT in schools, without defining the term, licenses parents to complain about any race-related lessons that make their children "feel uncomfortable." The Keller, Texas school district, a suburban town outside Dallas-Fort Worth, removed *The Diary of Anne Frank* from its schools because a parent complained that reading about Anne Frank's discomforts in an Amsterdam attic through much of World War II made her child uncomfortable. Hazara teenage girls restricted from high school in Kabul are reading *The Diary* together in a Kabul basement precisely because it speaks to their own experience under Taliban control, certainly more uncomfortable than a white middle-class Texas schoolgirl's. Georgia has outlawed teaching "divisive concepts" in class. Parents, employees, and college students are effectively being deputized by the state to enforce the law, updating historical practices of elevating whites to police Black and Brown people and their supporters. In Virginia, Governor Youngkin established a "tipline" for parents to report (racially) "divisive lessons" in schools. In all these cases, the charge itself is the penalty, for even if false, the social damage to career, to social standing, to education more broadly, has already been done. James Whitfield in Texas was a victim of just such a complaint, if from a by-standing adult. This, too, is deregulating racism in process.

The misleadingly reductive attacks on CRT, as well as those on Marxism, are key to this broader undertaking to deregulate. At the heart of neoliberalization has been the commitment to wipe out economic regulation by the state while ramping up socio-political and cultural restriction. "Marxism" is the characterization directed at all regulation conservatives find constraining. Castigating "CRT" is designed both to free up any expression they feel inclined to promote, including racist speech and action, while placing progressives on the defensive regarding individual freedoms. The license to say or do anything is paired with regulating any expression determined disagreeable.

The current targeting of schools amplifies this four-decade neoliberalization. It seeks to undermine trust in public schooling if not eliminate it altogether, to pull schooling out from under state regulation. Rufo, using his Fox News platform access, has been working with others to "liberate" education funding to support universal parental school choice. Their aim is to free up funding not just for charter or private religious schools but for the dark-money takeover of education more generally. Even arcade mall micro-schools that evade any state accreditation requirements are to be funded. The drive is to replace public schooling as the basis for a broadly common culture with the parochialisms, largely racially profiled, of one's narrowed interest groups. The Hillsdale College charter school initiative is but the foot in the door. The targeting of CRT, then, and what Rufo is now characterizing as "cultural Marxism," is a stepping-stone to school re-segregation and right-wing "invasion" and "takeover" of public universities. It is the project of narrowcasting and maleducating America.[15]

*

The cacophony of racial dismissal since September 2020 has all emanated from the Rufo crowd. It has placed on the defensive, where not silencing, both critical race theorists and those concerned with a responsible race-critical historical memory. It has tried to silence any analysis of racial conditions that might focus on redress or reparations. The silenced tend not to disappear. They go underground, become invisible to regroup and recharge.

I grew up in apartheid South Africa, completing my schooling there. Anything remotely critical of apartheid and its history of production was prohibited. My circle of friends and I spent our teenage years scavenging for exactly those materials. Well before stumbling across Asimov, we knew that a book that has to be banned is a book that must be read. Any time associates went abroad, they were given a list of readings with which to return, packed away discreetly between clothing. Once in our hands the materials were hungrily circulated in our group, and secretly discussed. Curious kids pursue exactly those materials officials seek to deny them, not least those explaining why authorities are driven to rule by division and political repression.

We are seeing the re-stirrings of a more assertive critical counter, from the ground up. Here is one example, in response to the Tennessee case regarding Ruby Bridges' book, mentioned earlier: "[O]ur teachers [in the Tennessee school district] are reporting to us that our students are reading like they've never read before." Because of the non-whitewashed history that the students are being provided with, the assistant school super-intendent added that "I've received a flood of emails recently that said, 'Don't do anything with the curriculum. My kid's loving it'."

The resistance is growing creative. School teenagers across America are mobilizing to get bans overturned. Children's curiosity has been spiked. Local bookstores are stocking up on ban-listed books, their sales and loan copy circulation soaring. As in Kabul, a Pennsylvania fourteen-year-old, with her parent's support, teamed up with a bookshop to start a Teen Banned Books Club to read and discuss books banned by school boards around the country. The restricted books are being read much more widely than before they were targeted.[16] Black parents in the hundreds, especially, are organizing counter-groups to ensure America's history and literature are not racially or gender cleansed in these attempted purges. UCLA Law School's seminal Critical Race Theory Program has introduced a tracking system to identify and analyze legisla-tive restrictions of CRT and "truthful information about . . . systemic racism."[17] They are committed to surfacing the sys-tematic censorship of CRT.

The whitewashing by Trufer-inspired watchlists is not just censorious, sloppy, and misdirecting. It is, of course, com-pletely reasonable for parents to be concerned about what their children are being taught at school. However, this does not entail that a small group of parents should dictate to a school or district at large what can or cannot be taught. There are already mechanisms in place for parents to contest school materials, which generally operate quite well. While censoring curricula may make for effective propagandistic politicking and clickbait, in the homogeneous circles in which it circu-lates it amounts to boring, unappealing, mostly misinformed, tuned-out pedagogy. It is *critical* in that other, fast failing sense.

The CRT problem, for Trufers, is the old "Negro problem" dressed up in fancy terms. The problem is *not* CRT. It is Rufo's fabrication. This is compounded by the fact that Rufo and his co-conspirators have started to believe their own make-believe. Success, in the sense of take-up, has collapsed any distance between design of the code and unquestioning investment in supposing its truth-value. The troubling implication of deregulating racism becomes insistence on historical ignorance, impactless legacies, on white innocence.[18]

There has been a sharp increase since 2020 of attempts to ban anti-racist books from school use.[19] Thinking and learning are quite literally being closed down. If Trufers refuse to read anything that might give them an inkling of Black heterogeneous history and life, they might spend a couple of hours watching the great Questlove documentary, *Summer of Soul*. Accompanying the fabulous music – yes, there's more gospel than almost any other musical fare on tap – they will find in it, as the Harlem Cultural Festival producer Tony Lawrence puts it in the film, their "first fifteen minutes of Black history." If none of this grabs them, they are, quite frankly, unsalvageable. It is one thing being uninformed oneself. That is just outright ignorance. It is something else again to demand that everyone else remain, by social policy, completely ignorant too.

*

Calling the broad legacy of racial covenants "structural" or "systemic racism" clearly riles Trufers. One can just as well define it as enduring racism. The enduring nature is enabled by social structures and cultural ways of being, social presumptions and norms not yet dismantled and deleted. They tend to endure even where individual people, even most, become less prejudiced or discriminatory. While there are obviously differences between the legacies of racism in the U.S. and within and across European states, what I am pointing to by way of "enduring racism" continues to mark these formations. To ensure structural racisms endure appear to be Trufism's founding commitment and continued investment. To reveal and counter these logics and social impacts, by contrast, have been the critical driving points of CRT, from the outset.

Rufo sensed that the older ways were slipping. He conspired with the Trufists to "push back," composing racial distortions designed to unsettle, even scare whites. Trufism's setting out to execute Critical Race Theory, in the killing sense, may have had some short-term success. Yet it has helped, counter-intuitively, to pull into the open the necessity of a more open, honest engagement around racisms and their histories. There are, to riff off Marvin Gaye again, still too many brothers and sisters dying.

Unaddressed, racism tends to reproduce itself, become irrepressible. It exhausts, beats its targets down, still can kill. Postracial or raceless racism tends to focus on individual racist expression, a culture of accusation confining itself over-whelmingly to individual agency rather than the structures perpetuating a racist social system. Calling out individual racism is not unimportant. Left unaddressed, proliferating individual racism serves to perpetuate structures of racism. As Patricia Williams urged nearly three decades ago, sometimes one really has to break up a good party.

Nevertheless, it is better, on balance, to say of an expression or action rather than an individual that it is racist, unless especially and unapologetically so, or an extension of a pattern by the person in question. The challenge is to turn individual racist expression into a learning opportunity, for the perpetrator, and generally. Ideally, this would be graciously composed, inviting those less inclined to hear and accept the critical lessons rather than "walling them out." It is no doubt imperative to call out a racist as racist. Where egregious and unapologetic, racist expression and institutional operation require firm responses. Where done well, though, an open, productive discussion about racisms and their overcoming would more readily re-position the accused into a partnering advocate for justice than an embittered and resistant pariah.

Bright Sheng survived the Cultural Revolution in China as a boy. A globally notable composer and MacArthur Fellow awardee, he is a distinguished professor at the University of Michigan. On the first day of in-person classes in Fall 2021, following eighteen months of pandemic lockdown, he sought to demonstrate for undergraduate students the cinematic power of music. He showed the 1965 film, *Othello*, starring Laurence Olivier. Providing no context for the production, he was concerned only that the students be moved by the impact of Verdi's score. Olivier, it is widely known, plays Othello in blackface. The students were deeply unsettled. While the reporting focused exclusively on his face coloring, perhaps the students were disturbed by more than this. Already in a 1966 review the *New York Times* had raised concerns about racial stereotyping, including Olivier's "kinky black hair" wig and thickly reddened lips.[20] Professor Sheng had established no relation yet with the students, no basis for trust. Upon their complaints, to him and the department's administration, he apologized, if at first awkwardly, repeating his remorse as the controversy ballooned.

Wanting to look like it was doing the right thing, the department faculty and administration removed Sheng from teaching the course. Sheng has pointedly expressed interest in learning productively from the experience, rather than, as in too many other cases, recalcitrance and resistance to change. Cases and individuals differ. The students exhibited rightful impatience at having to experience another indignity, and rising indignation at the professor's failure to self-inform about a matter of deep concern. This is not "woke racism" so much as generationally shifting standards, and here justifiably so.

Where a person shows remorse and looks to do better, nevertheless, finding ways to enable that possibility rather than persisting with accusation seems far more productive. Cultivating solidarities will help more than alienation over the long haul. When personal vilification becomes the endgame, it reproduces the culture of individualization, reducing racisms to agency, thus losing sight of social structure. That's exactly the logic represented by the too-quick reach for MLK's one line about being just about character over color. It's exactly the terrain on which Trufers want to fight.

Perhaps a case like Sheng's might enable structural change, here at the departmental or institutional level. It says a great deal that undergraduate students were altogether more familiar with the issues of concern than the instructor. There is a distinction to hold onto between addressable failure to know and making a virtue of ignorance (Rufo and company have repeatedly demonstrated willful ignorance). Protocols might be established where racially (in)sensitive or problematic material is to be taught, requiring that the instructor discuss how best to do so with the department at large (or, in schools, with other teachers, including those of color). All faculty would learn and students benefit from the exercise, developing collectively from hearing non-defensively about sensitivities, insights, and concerns at issue. Structural transformation requires different ways of thinking and doing, from the ground up. Not all cases will qualify, some still out of bounds and requiring stronger responses. Structural elements do not forego judgment, which likewise requires careful cultivation.

Social trust, clearly, has been destroyed, on all sides of these divides. This destruction is an extension of Trumpist logic, to encourage general social distrust: in government and the state (attacks on "the swamp" and "deep state"), in voting and election outcomes, in science (regarding the pandemic, effects of social distancing, masking, and vaccines, not to mention the causes of climate change). The impact has been to sew radical distrust in each other, and ultimately in any sort of legitimate authority, to clear the way for autocratic rule. Trufism, using the attacks on CRT as its weaponized battering ram, is the latest extension of this reach. The Trufer aim has been to undermine authority in educational institutions, a key stepping-stone to deregulating racism. The question is how best to reinstate trust, first and foremost in open processes of truth-making and collective verifiability[21] as well as in a sense of mutually respectful and dignified learning from each other. To learn together from our actual histories of co-formation, in all their fraught and intersecting co-constitutions, pains and pleasures.

Recreating conditions that would engender trust requires thinking about cultivating socially supporting virtues and their consistent application, not least regarding racial matters. The aim is to encourage sustained *curiosity* both in what we all share and in our histories of distinctive if relational formings, even, and perhaps especially, where painful; to fashion a *humility* about our own histories, what has made us, mindful of our social standing and, whatever that standing, of the limits of our knowledge and power; to develop *integrity* as a sustaining investment in the value of honesty over deceit and denial; and an openness to *sharing*, in dignified ways, the critical together with the celebratory.[22]

*

Trufism is both distraction from and reversal of the commitment to addressing and redressing racisms and their remainders. As distraction, it draws attention away from recognizing racisms when they occur. And as reversal, Trufism is designed to liberate and license racist expression unhindered by any regulatory restriction.

CRT 1.0 focuses on considerations of structural racism. Responses by DiAngelo and others, however, are reminders that there is slippage, sometimes all too readily, into offering responses at the level of individual agency that leave the structural unaddressed. The recent stress on "unconscious bias" again leans in this direction. At their most engaging and trenchantly insightful, Critical Race Theory and Critical Race Studies are commitments to how we might together go about productively transforming our society, structurally and culturally. It is not that individual racisms, like expressions of unconscious bias, are unimportant. The structural and individual reinforce each other. And yet, the reduction to individuated expression leaves the structural untouched. The pressing undertaking is to move us to social institutions and culture more fully, openly, and invitingly representative of racial justice and social heterogeneity. That is the executing of critical race analysis in the sense of effectively carrying out Martin Luther King's fully fledged Dream.

Any state of equals requires that its members be taken seriously, have a baseline of sustaining material support, be treated with dignity, and enjoy the reasonable opportunity to pursue, advance, and contribute to others in their chosen endeavors. In its broader vision, CRT helped to open up an extensive set of reflections and debates about what these aspirational goals look like and how to achieve them, often in the face of both academic and public hostility. The debate has been as messy among proponents as with critics. But the messiness doesn't detract from the necessity, nor from the sometime impacts, far less likely to have been brought about but for the messy interventions.

That we are at some distance from those goals still, and facing hostility as vehement as ever, indicates the driving need for what CRT best represents. That need is palpable even as the analyses to which it is committed develop and transform in the face of the changing political-economic landscape. In this, it tends to differ from public-facing scholarship in other fields in one crucial respect. Because race pervades the social, race-critical analysis remains a key component of all especially public scholarship. That requires also being mindful of saying sometimes difficult things absolutely clearly, in ways less open to be twisted to counter-purpose, as we have seen Trufists all too ready to do.

Since the mid-twentieth century formative national accounts of race and racism in America were released at approximately twenty-five-year intervals. The publications were followed by vigorous national discussion. Gunnar Myrdal's copious study, *An American Dilemma: The Negro Problem and Modern Democracy* (1944) set this process going. The Kerner Commission's take on "Two Americas" followed in 1968, updated in turn by Andrew Hacker a quarter century later (I discussed the latter two briefly in Part I). There are now, as Ishmael Reed has phrased it, "multi-Americas," not just two. While there have been many micro-studies of race and racism in the thirty years since Hacker's, there has been no capacious national study comparable to these earlier ones, which regarded the different Americas racially inhabited, and the extraordinary contributions made to the making of the nation despite the daunting challenges faced. It would contribute significantly to an honest, openly verifiable national self-portrait of American racial experience today, ranging across material and socially mediated conditions.

Such a comprehensive study, in turn, would furnish a framework for a robust, open discussion of what a Reconstruction for our times would address and amount to. The driving questions concern how racially prompted injurious property loss might be redressed; how housing, social infrastructures, and health care would serve all people rather than profit-making; how school resources, learning support, and work training might be debtlessly equalized and updated for the world today; and how law and its application might be transformed to support rather than curtail or deny fully realized lives for all.

*

Christopher Rufo is the driving representative of the approach to racism I have called Trufism, addressing only individual action, while committed to deregulating racism in the name of being nominally against it. Kimberlé Crenshaw represents the best of CRT, the antithesis to Trufism. They each stand for contrasting ways of *seeing* and *being* in the world. We can close by asking what is being done by the movements with which they are each associated to advance racial justice.

For one, teachers are being fired, historical books about integrating public schools are being banned from schools, pernicious racisms are circulating with giddy abandonment, death threats multiplying. For the other, political actors, policy makers, and police are being called to account for structures and actions giving rise to, or extending, violence and killings to which racially positioned populations continue to be overwhelmingly rendered prone.

Those moved by Rufo and his anti-CRT rant take one to be solely what one makes of oneself and the mostly equal opportunities all social actors supposedly can exploit. Social advancement is considered not anymore limited by racial structure.[23] Crenshaw is a key figure in a collective undertaking to keep the focus on how systemic racism structures the state, its institutions and culture. Rufo has mobilized others to maintain white control over the racial agenda in the country, most notably regarding the school curriculum. Crenshaw, like her mentor Derrick Bell, has always been committed to advancing justice for those historically and contemporarily most subjugated and disenfranchised.

As we have seen, Trufism deregulates and so encourages individual racism, making people feel more entitled to express themselves in recognizably and unapologetically racist ways. Deregulating racism seeks to undercut if not altogether to undo the impacts of, and indeed insight into, the history of anti-racism, laid out in Chapter 3 above, from abolitionism to Black Lives Matter and renewed reaches for reconstruction. Deregulated, individual racism running rampant reinforces the structural and systemic, informally keeping the entitlements, advantages, and powers established by them firmly in place. Structure and agency require each other for their co-perpetuation.

Trufism and its proponents will come and go, replaced by some other mode of retrenchment, given the shoddiness of the current efforts. It is but the latest fad of racial negation. Deregulating racism, however, is likely to have a more extended shelf life, precisely because it structures anew the possibility of racisms socially unaddressed, if not unrecognized. A social life of dignity and respect for all, contrastingly, requires not just recognition as equals but addressing the conditions for both formal and substantive, structural and individual equality.

Critical Race Theory remains faithful to the Kantian critical tradition of baring the contradictions and antinomies in all thinking, and to Frantz Fanon's abiding commitment to keep questioning. When properly practiced, in both its legal and more capacious social applications, CRT is as necessary as when first founded for understanding fully our collective and relational histories. It is critical for addressing the scope of enduring racisms, and how by embodying racial justice honestly we can forge interactive, mutually engaging, generative, and rewarding lives fully together.

Harry Frankfurt compares "bullshit" to lying. Liars comprehend that they are misrepresenting the truth. They work to hide or cover over the trail of their misrepresentations. Bullshitters, however, show no regard for whether their assertions have any truth-value. They are concerned only that their target audience is persuaded.[24] Rufo and his Trumpian co-travelers, like Mark Levin, Ted Cruz, and Ron DeSantis, appear less concerned with the truth of their claims than with whether most will believe their fabrications and act as they would want them to as a result. Like Trump, they are invested in their own make-believe, believing that believing is all that counts. Bullshit is out to rule:

the event, the day, the historical period inhabited, history itself. Complaining bitterly that all others have given up on the truth of race, they are the first to flaunt it, and to do so without conscience.

Conservatives have complained increasingly loudly of their exhaustion at the incessant accusations of racism. They might take that as a small indication of what life is like for racisms' targets, present and past. Rather than address the root social causes, this new conservativism undertakes to regulate anti-racism to silence the source of their irritation. Racial strife has structured political economy and civil society since the onset of modernity and the founding of the Republic: slavery and abolition, colonialism, the Civil War; segregation, immigration codes, Jim Crow; the Civil Rights and anti-apartheid struggles, racial neoliberalization; racially profiled poverty, policing, and prison abolition.

There is a deeper, less clearly articulated struggle being played out in our time. On one side are those more-or-less vocally wanting to maintain or return to an unregulated racial status quo, socially and institutionally, with some open to a smattering around the edges of add-on diversity, pedagogically and culturally. This is the sociality colorblindness envisages. On the other side are those committed to a far more robust sense of structural justice and social equality. Here the concern is to address, educationally and socially, the legacy of inequalities that racisms have structured enduringly into the social system. This, not too-quick colorblindness, is Martin Luther King's legacy:

> I never intend to adjust myself to segregation and discrimination. I never intend to become adjusted to a religious bigotry. I never intend to adjust myself to economic conditions that will take necessities from the many to give luxuries to the few, leaving millions of people smothering in an air-tight cage of poverty in the midst of an affluent society. I never intend

to adjust myself to the madness of militarism and the self-defeating effects of physical violence.[25]

Perhaps Trufer parents will want to ban King too on the grounds he produces the discomforts of their children's rebelliousness. Rufo and his crowd can spit into the gale all they want. Until we compose the grounds for a state of full equality, the analytic toolbox for which Critical Race Theory stands will remain key.

James Baldwin closes his prescient essay, "Stranger in the Village," by pointing out that

> This world is white no longer, and it will never be white again.[26]

The attacks on CRT are desperately seeking to hold onto or reproduce their old world as the new one takes hold. Martin Luther King's Dream, by contrast, reaches for a more justly and jointly structured state predicated on mutual dignity and recognizing equals. There is a whole lot more to be gained from living with those not mirror images than with clones of oneself. A social life of anti-violent co-existence is predicated not on "owning others" but on owning up to the mutual virtues and values only living in a robustly heterogeneous culture can enable. In place of fear from loss of control, a gun and a beating always the default, Trufers might just try turning their backs to the cracked mirror, the fever swamp echo chamber of social media, and face life as it is in all its exciting variation. The stark choice facing us today: grappling with the messy if elevating challenges of an increasingly mixed world; or turning us into Stasi-like informers incessantly prying on neighbors and fellow-workers. To give up on trying to secure or exercise absolute control is to gain worlds. Living freely is a life *with*, not against others.

It is this more expansive Dream for which Critical Race

Theory reaches too. The reach for freedom, within and across worlds. To *be* free, and equal, at last.

Acknowledgments

This book is a product of the politics of our time. But it could not have been written without decades of engagement and exchanges around both Critical Race Theory and Critical Race Studies. There are far too many to name who have paved the way, and many are referenced in the book.

More directly, I am indebted to those without whom the book likely would not have materialized, at least not in the terms outlined here. Robin Kelley kindly opened the door to *Boston Review* to place initial thoughts about the attacks against CRT on their platform. *BR* spared no effort in turning the essay into uncontestable form. Similarly, Chauncey DeVega connected me with *Salon*, which published a follow-up piece. The writing of the book began to take shape as a consequence of these publications.

My dear friend, colleague, and neighbor, Aaron James, read early drafts of the book, pushing me to clarify and simplify. While a different book from the drafts he read, the current one would not have taken shape but for his insights. Anjali Prabhu and Lisa Leung both raised questions about earlier drafts and led to revisions.

Barbara Ransom arranged my presentation in workshops with the Pennsylvania Bar Association and Philadelphia District Attorney office. I learned a great deal from the exchanges with other presenters, including Barbara, Anjali Vats, and Judge Donald Hahn, as well as from workshop participants. Extensive discussion throughout the writing of the book with Anirban Gupta-Nigam led to insights and details that otherwise would have passed me by. Rachel Rosenfelt and Douglas Rushkoff, co-conspirators on another project, pushed me to publication in all the moments of self-doubt. Philomena Essed endured my daily exasperation over the misreperesentations of CRT and the contorted politics they were being advanced to effect. As always, discussions with her opened up for me ways of thinking otherwise hidden from view.

Jonathan Skerrett, my editor at Polity, encouraged clarification and refinement of every idea while shepherding me carefully through to production. The Polity staff, as always, have smoothed out the production process in terrifically supportive ways. I am grateful also to two anonymous reviewers for their insights and ideas for improving on earlier drafts.

Notes

Preface

1 David Theo Goldberg, "The War on Critical Race Theory," *Boston Review*, May 7, 2021. https://bostonreview.net/articles/the-war -on-critical-race-theory/

David Theo Goldberg, "Meet Christopher Rufo," *Salon*, August 1, 2021. https://www.salon.com/2021/08/01/meet-christopher-ru fo--leader-of-the-incoherent-right-wing-attack-on-critical-race -theory/

2 Victor Ray, *On Critical Race Theory: Why It Matters and Why You Should Care*. Random House, 2022.

3 Cf. In addition to Victor Ray's book: Stuart Hall et al. *Policing the Crisis: Mugging the State, and Law and Order*. Palgrave, 1978; Martin Barker, *The New Racism*. Junction Books, 1981.

1 What's Going On?

1 David Theo Goldberg, *Dread: Facing Futureless Futures*. Polity, 2021.

2 The 1619 Project is an initiative by journalist Nikole Hannah-Jones and the *New York Times* to center slavery in the teaching of American history. It has generated extraordinary controversy, and became a principal target at school board protests.

See https://pulitzercenter.org/lesson-plan-grouping/1619-pro ject-curriculum and Adam Server, "The fight over the 1619 project is not about the facts," *The Atlantic*, December 23, 2019. https:// www.theatlantic.com/ideas/archive/2019/12/historians-clash-16 19-project/604093/

3 Federal Register, "Combatting race and sex stereotyping," September 28, 2021. https://www.federalregister.gov/documents /2020/09/28/2020-21534/combating-race-and-sex-stereotyping

2 The Headliners

1 Christopher Rufo, "Chris Rufo calls media denial CRT exists in schools a 'deliberate strategy': 'They have no choice' but to lie," Fox News, November 5, 2021. https://www.foxnews.com/media /christopher-rufo-media-critical-race-theory

2 Mike Gonzalez, *The Plot to Change America: How Identity Politics is Dividing the Land of the Free*. Encounter Books, 2020.

3 Richard Hasen, *American Meltdown: Dirty Tricks, Distrust, and the Threat to American Democracy*. Yale University Press, 2020.

4 Nicholas Riccardi and Anthony Izaguirre, "Conservative group boasts of secret role in voting laws," *AP News*, May 14, 2021. https://apnews.com/article/politics-donald-trump-laws-voting -government-and-politics-c07c55f7dd3ad5847d31d7a5123b b82c

5 Judd Legum, *Twitter*, July 20, 2021. https://twitter.com/juddle gum/status/1414928964326412294?lang=en

6 Alyce McFadden, "Secretive 'dark money' network launches anti-critical race theory campaign," *openSecrets*, June 30, 2021. https://www.opensecrets.org/news/2021/06/secretive-dark-money-network-anti-critical-race-theory/

7 *City Journal*, https://www.city-journal.org/search?searchterms= critical%20race%20theory

8 Heritage Foundation, *Critical Race Theory Legislation Tracker*, heritage.org. https://datavisualizations.heritage.org/education /critical-race-theory-legislation-tracker/

9 Stephanie Saul, "Energizing conservative voters, one school board election at a time," *New York Times*, October 21, 2021.

10 Freitas identifies earlier twentieth-century German sociologists Max Weber and Georg Simmel as among the CRT-influencing critical theorists. Neither was a Marxist. While both bodies of work were seriously discussed by the school of thought identified as Critical Theory, that simply identifies the nature of serious scholarly work, not identity of thought in a common school. https://twitter.com/NickForVA/status/1443395119328137222

11 https://citizensrenewingamerica.com/

12 https://citizensrenewingamerica.com/issues/combatting-critic al-race-theory-in-your-community/

13 https://citizensrenewingamerica.com/issues/model-school-board -language-to-prohibit-critical-race-theory-2/

14 https://www.reclaimingourschools.com/

15 https://legalinsurrectionfoundation.org/

16 https://criticalrace.org/

17 https://1776unites.com/essays/our-open-letter-to-public-school -boards/

18 http://nebula.wsimg.com/9499c73d959b9f49be9689476a990776 ?AccessKeyId=45A6F09DA41DB93D9538&disposition=0&allo worigin=1

19 David Horowitz, *I Can't Breathe: How a Racial Hoax Is Killing America*. Regnery Publishing, 2021.

20 Voddie Baucham, "Critical race theory: The fault lines of social justice," Heritage Foundation, June 10, 2021. https://www.herit age.org/progressivism/event/virtual-critical-race-theory-the-fau lt-lines-social-justice

21 As a racial metaphor, "colorblindness" is the declared refusal to make or recognize racial distinctions. "Blindness," as disability studies analysts have pointed out, often carries pejorative presumption. Those asserting racial colorblindness take themselves to be committed to an affirming racial practice. It would be difficult to address this commitment critically without use of the term, mindful nevertheless of the disability studies concerns.

3 Critical Race Theory

1 Kerner Commission Report on The Causes, Events, and Aftermaths of the Civil Disorders Of 1967, U.S. Department of Justice, 1967. https://www.ojp.gov/ncjrs/virtual-library/abstracts/national-advisory-commission-civil-disorders-report

2 William Julius Wilson, *The Declining Significance of Race.* University of Chicago Press, 1978.

3 Stuart Hall, "Race, articulations, and societies structured in dominance," in *Sociological Theories: Race and Colonialism,* pp. 305–345. UNESCO, 1980.

4 Andrew Hacker, *Two Nations: Black and White, Separate, Hostile, and Unequal.* Scribner, 1992.

5 Orlando Patterson's notable study, *Slavery and Social Death,* sought to place the history of American slavery in wider global and historical context. Consider also the eminent scholarship of David Brion Davis, Barbara Fields, Philip Foner, Eric Foner, Eugene Genovese, Catherine Hall, Nell Painter, and Marcus Rediker, among others.

6 This work was led by Stephen Jay Gould, Nancy Leys Stepan, and Richard Lewontin.

7 Prominent contributors to the critical philosophy of race at the time included Etienne Balibar, Anthony Appiah, Cornel West, Angela Davis, the New York Society for the Study of Black Philosophy, and Adrien Piper's philosophical and art practice.

8 Compare the London-based journal *Race and Class,* the work of Robert Miles, Manning Marable, and Michael Omi and Howard's Winant's popularizing of the notion of "racial formation." It was in the mid-1980s, too, that Cedric Robinson launched his impactful analysis of "racial capitalism," influenced by spending time in Southern Africa.

9 Patricia Hill Collins made accessible the range of Black feminist thinking. Philomena Essed focused on "everyday racism," the term she coined. Hazel Carby analyzed conditions of race, gender, and power. bell hooks at the time brought to attention the terror of whiteness for those not white. And Colette

Guillaumin added reflections in the French context on racism, sexism, and domination.

10 Stuart Hall's seminal contributions centered race in Cultural Studies from the mid-1970s on, and proved enormously impactful in producing a generation of scholarship, including most notably Paul Gilroy's. In the mid-1980s, Henry Louis Gates, Jr. shaped the field of race and literary studies with Barbara Christian, Hortense Spillers, Toni Morrison, and Houston Baker. Gates and Appiah's *"Race," Writing and Difference*, an expansive volume of key new writings on race and racism, laid a substantial foundation for these new directions.

11 Richard Dyer in Britain opened up the field of whiteness studies, with significant transatlantic impact. At the same time, Angela Davis and David Roediger spoke to the ways race, class, and, in Davis's case, gender reinforced each other in American society. These were followed by studies of how, once ethnoracially maligned immigrant groups to the U.S. – the Irish (Theodore Allen, Noel Ignatiev), Jews (Karen Brodkin), and Italians (Jennifer Guglielmo) – had historically "become white."

12 W.E.B. Du Bois, *The Philadelphia Negro*. University of Pennsylvania Press, 1995.

13 See David Roediger, *Towards the Abolition of Whiteness*, Verso Books, 1994, p. 29.

14 Eduardo Bonilla-Silva, *Racism without Racists: Color-Blind Racism and the Persistence of Racial Inequality in America*. Rowman and Littlefield, 1997.

15 Kimberlé Crenshaw, "Mapping the margins: Intersectionality, identity politics, and violence against women of color," in Crenshaw et al., eds. *Critical Race Theory: The Key Writings that Formed the Movement*, pp. 357–383. The Free Press, 1995.

16 Carol Anderson, *The Second: Race and Guns in a Fatally Unequal America*. Bloomsbury, 2021.

17 Christopher Rufo, *Critical Race Theory Briefing Book*. https://christopherrufo.com/crt-briefing-book/

4 A Method of Misreading

1 Christopher Rufo, "Critical race theory." https://www.youtube
.com/watch?v=cfmpnGV0IGc

2 Christopher Rufo, *Critical Race Theory Briefing Book*. https://
christopherrufo.com/crt-briefing-book/

3 https://twitter.com/realchrisrufo/status/1371541044592996352
?lang=en

4 Laura Meckler and Josh Dawsey, "Republicans, spurred by an
unlikely figure, see political promise in targeting critical race
theory," *Washington Post*, June 21, 2021.

5 The Southern Strategy was developed by Republicans such as
Goldwater and Nixon from the mid-1960s on to mobilize white
voters in the American South by proposing racist policies disadvantaging and running advertizing campaigns vilifying African
Americans.

6 D'Souza was convicted of unlawful campaign funding and
then lying about it, spending time in a half-way house and on
probation. He was pardoned by Trump as he departed the
Presidency.

7 Sam Hoadley-Brill, a philosophy graduate student, points out on
Twitter this latter mode of proceeding too. https://twitter.com/de
onteleologist/status/1402278740269449224?lang=en).%20Q.E.D.

5 ~~Structural Racism?~~

1 Kaelan Deese, "Byron Donalds says critical race theory wants to
'trap' people by 'the scars of our nation'," *Washington Examiner*,
July 21, 2021.

2 Brooke Staggs, "Larry Elder talks racism, school choice and
repealing COVID mandates," *Orange County Register*, August
21, 2021; Meaghan Ellis, "Mississippi Governor designates April
as Confederate History Month," *Salon*, April 14, 2022. https://
www.salon.com/2022/04/14/mississippi-governor-designates
-april-as-heritage-month_partner/

3 Larry Elder, "No evidence of anti-Black systemic racism," *The
Joplin Globe*, April 12, 2021. https://www.joplinglobe.com/opin

ion/columns/larry-elder-no-evidence-of-anti-black-systemic-racism/article_cedff786-97ee-11eb-829d-737cd6512025.html

4   For the redlining California maps and supporting materials, see "T-Races: http://t-races.net/T-RACES/

5   Alicia Victoria Lozano, "California moves to return property seized from Black couple," NBC News, September 10, 2021. https://www.nbcnews.com/news/nbcblk/california-moves-retu rn-bruce-s-beach-seized-black-couple-n1278931

6   For a general reparative argument, see William Darity, Jr. and A. Kirsten Mullen, *From Here to Equality: Reparations for Black Americans in the 21st Century.* University of North Carolina Press, 2020.

7   Haley M. Lane et al., "Historical redlining is associated with present-day air pollution disparities in U.S. cities," ACS Publications, March 9, 2022 https://pubs.acs.org/doi/10.1021/acs.estlett.1c0 1012

8   Nathan Nunn et al., "After the burning: The economic effects of the 1921 Tulsa Massacre." https://scholar.harvard.edu/nunn /publications/after-burning-economic-effects-1921-tulsa-race -massacre

9   Debra Kamin, "Home appraised with a Black owner: $472,000. With a white owner: $750,000," *New York Times*, August 18, 2022. https://www.nytimes.com/2022/08/18/realestate/housing -discrimination-maryland.html

10 FEANTSA, "FEANTSA's input for the United Nations Special Rapporteur on housing discrimination and spatial segregation," 14 May, 2021. https://www.ohchr.org › Housing › FEANTSA
    European Network Against Racism, "Racism and discrimination in employment, 2013–17." https://www.enar-eu.org/ 2013-17-enar-shadow-report-on-racism-and-discrimination-in-employment-in-europe/

11 Mark R. Levin, *American Marxism.* Threshold Editions, 2021, p. 116.

12 Board of Governors of Federal Reserve System, "Disparities in wealth by race and ethnicity in the 2019 Survey of Consumer

Finances," September 28, 2020. https://www.federalreserve.gov/econres/notes/feds-notes/disparities-in-wealth-by-race-and-ethnicity-in-the-2019-survey-of-consumer-finances-20200928.htm

13 *ACLU Magazine*, Fall 2021, p. 18.

14 Charles Mills, Interview with Laura Basu, *openVoices*, September 16, 2020. https://www.opendemocracy.net/en/oureconomy/charles-mills-there-opening-transracial-class-alliance/

15 Cheryl Harris, "Whiteness as property," *Harvard Law Review*, June 10, 1993.

16 This, of course, might be reversed, given the current composition of the Supreme Court, and the affirmative action case now before it: *Students for Fair Admissions vs. Harvard University*.

17 On the dual significance of "de-meaning," see David Theo Goldberg, *Dread: Facing Futureless Futures*, Polity, 2021, pp. 30–31.

6 The Gospel of Colorblindness

1 Anita Little, " Buried Truths," *ACLU Magazine*, Fall 2021, pp. 16–21.

2 This formulation is drawn from the CACAGNY documents introduced in Chapter 3 but represents a widely held Trufist characterization; italics in the original.

3 There are, of course, significant differences, historically and contemporarily, colonially and postcolonially, between the ways in which EU states address racism. Religious differences between northern and southern European states and regions, the impact on the forms of secularism that emerged from them, distinctions between universalisms and nationalisms are crucial to bear in mind for any comprehensive analysis of European-wide approaches to racism. Post World War II, however, the EU has been increasingly driven by a comprehensive commitment to state non-racialism, or what I generically characterize as racelessness.

4 Carolynn Look, "Black people in German survey report 'extensive' discrimination," *Bloomberg*, November 30, 2021. https://www.

bloomberg.com/news/articles/2021-11-30/black-people-in-ger
man-survey-report-extensive-discrimination#xj4y7vzkg

5 Patricia Williams, *Seeing a Color-Blind Future: The Paradox of Race* (BBC Reith Lectures). Farrar, Strauss and Giroux, 1998. Kimberlé Williams Crenshaw et al., eds. *Seeing Race Again: Countering Colorblindness Across the Disciplines.* University of California Press, 2019.

6 *Plessy v. Ferguson,* 163 U.S. 537 (1896).

7 Supreme Court of the U.S.A., *Shelby County, Alabama v. Holder, Attorney General et al.,* No. 12–96, Argued February 27, 2013, Decided June 25, 2013.

8 Heritage Foundation, "The case for color-blindness," Report, September 6, 2019. The Report affirmingly quotes Harlan's defense of colorblindness. https://www.heritage.org/civil-society /report/the-case-color-blindness

9 Philomena Essed, "Entitlement racism and its intersections: An interview with Philomena Essed," *ephemera: theory and politics in organization* 18 (1), 2018: 183–201. http://www.ephemerajour nal.org/sites/default/files/pdfs/contribution/18-1essedmuhr.pdf

7 Fictive Histories

1 Christopher Rufo, "Critical race theory: What it is and how to fight it," Imprimis: Hillsdale College Newsletter, Vol. 50, No. 3, March 2021. https://imprimis.hillsdale.edu/critical-race-theory -fight/

2 Christopher F. Rufo, "Against wokeness: Conservatives must understand the threat posed by critical race theory," *City Journal,* September 16, 2020. https://www.city-journal.org/threat-of-cri tical-race-theory

3 From 1943 to 1950, Marcuse actually worked for the U.S. Office of Strategic Services, forerunner of the CIA. In a book published with the Office, he was scathingly critical of Soviet communism.

4 John Seely Brown and Douglas Thomas, "You play world of warcraft? You're hired! Why multiplayer games may be the best

kind of job training," *Wired*, April 1, 2006. https://www.wired
.com/2006/04/learn/

5 Kimberlé Crenshaw, Neil Gotanda, Gary Peller, and Kendall
Thomas, eds. *Critical Race Theory: The Key Writings that Formed
the Movement*. The New Press, 1995.

6 Richard Delgado, *Critical Race Theory: The Cutting Edge*. Temple
University Press, 1995; Richard Delgado and Jean Stefancic,
Critical Race Theory: An Introduction. New York University
Press, 2001. The latter is one of the books Ted Cruz waved in
the face of Judge Ketanji Brown Jackson during her Senate con-
firmation hearings for the Supreme Court, as if having attended
Harvard Law School she must have drunk the CRT Kool-Aid.

7 Danielle Pletka, Marc Thiessen, and Allen Guelzo, "WTH is
critical race theory? How a philosophy that inspired Marxism,
Nazism, and Jim Crow is making its way into our schools,
and what we can do," Episode #108, June 23, 2021. https://
www.aei.org/wp-content/uploads/2021/06/6.23.21-Guelzo-
transcript.pdf

In her testimony to the Senate Judicial Committee objecting to
Judge Jackson's nomination to the Supreme Court, conservative
lawyer Keisha Russell repeated Guelzo's mischaracterization of
Kant virtually verbatim. https://www.judiciary.senate.gov/imo
/media/doc/Russell%20KBJ%20Testimony.pdf

8 This latter claim is from Rufo-inspired documents publicly circulated nationally by the Chinese American Citizens Alliance
Greater New York (CACAGNY), introduced in Chapter 3
above.

9 Mitchell Dean and Daniel Zamora, *The Last Man Takes LSD:
Foucault and the End of Revolution*. Verso, 2021.

10 Mathew Campbell, "French philosopher Michel Foucault 'abused
boys in Tunisia'," *The Sunday Times* (London), March 28, 2021;
Centre Michel Foucault statement on Guy Sorman's accusations
against Michel Foucault and bibliography of Foucault in Tunisia,
Political Geographies, May 24, 2021. https://progressivegeograp
hies.com/2021/05/24/centre-michel-foucault-statement-on-guy

-sormans-accusations-against-michel-foucault-and-bibliogra
phy-of-foucault-in-tunisia/

11 Lithwick, Dahlia. "The Limbaugh Code: The *New York Times*
    best seller no one is talking about." *Slate*, April 1, 2005. Other
    commentators more recently are equally dismissive.

12 Levin, *American Marxism*, p. 159.

13 Levin, ibid., p. 105.

14 Levin, ibid.

15 David Theo Goldberg, "The power of tolerance," *Philosemitism,
    Antisemitism and the Jews: Perspectives from Antiquity to the
    Twentieth Century*, ed. by Tony Kushner, Sarah Pearce, and
    Nadia Valman, Ashgate Publishers, 2004.

16 Herbert Marcuse, "Repressive tolerance," in *A Critique of Pure
    Tolerance*, ed. by Robert Paul Wolff, Barrington Moore, and
    Herbert Marcuse. Beacon Press, 1965. https://la.utexas.edu/
    users/hcleaver/330T/350kPEEMarcuseToleranceTable.pdf

17 Eric Voegelin, *The History of the Race Idea: From Ray to Carus.
    Collected Works*, Vol. 3. University of Missouri Press. *Race and
    State. Collected Works*, Vol. 2. University of Missouri Press, 1997.
    Magnus Hirschfeld, *Racism*. Victor Gollancz, 1938. Voegelin fled
    the Nazis to the U.S., spending much of his career at Louisiana
    State University. Hirschfeld, Austrian too but practicing psychia-
    try in Berlin as the Nazis rose to power, also conceived of the
    term "transexual." He was targeted for persecution, fleeing to
    Switzerland, where he died in 1935.

18 Levin, *American Marxism*, pp. 8–14.

19 Ibid., p. 169.

20 George R. LaNoue, "Critical race training or civil rights law: We
    can't have both," *National Association of Scholars*, December 10,
    2020.   https://www.nas.org/blogs/article/critical-race-training
    -or-civil-rights-law-we-cant-have-both

21 Levin, *American Marxism*, p. 174.

22 Ibid. p. 175.

23 Ibid., pp. 175–176.

24 Christopher Rufo, "Chris Rufo calls media denial CRT exists in

schools a 'deliberate strategy': 'They have no choice' but to lie," Fox News, November 5, 2021. https://www.foxnews.com/media /christopher-rufo-media-critical-race-theory

25 Benjamin Wallace Wells, "How a Conservative activist invented the controversy over critical race theory," *New Yorker*, June 21, 2021.

26 Gabriella Borter, Joseph Ax, and Joseph Tanfani, "Schools under siege," A Reuters Special Report, February 15, 2022. https://www .reuters.com/investigates/special-report/usa-education-threats/

27 Mike Cole, *Critical Race Theory and Education*. Palgrave Macmillan, 2017; Charles Mills, "Critical race theory: A reply to Mike Cole," *Ethnicities* 9(2), 2009: 270–281.

28 Joshua Zitser, "Trump calls on supporters to 'lay down their very lives' to defend US against Critical Race Theory," *Business Insider*, March 13, 2022. https://www.businessinsider.com/video -trump-tells-supporters-lay-down-lives-battle-against-crt-2022 -3

8 Sounds of Silencing

1 Ibram X. Kendi, *Stamped from the Beginning: The Definitive History of Racist Ideas in America*. Bold Type Books, 2017; Kendi, *How to Be an Antiracist*. One World, 2019.

2 Robin DiAngelo, *White Fragility: Why it's so Hard for White People to Talk About Racism*. Beacon Press, 2018.

3 https://www.youtube.com/watch?v=ihnuYXKBGZg

4 https://www.youtube.com/watch?v=Y6vpygrwvUQ

5 https://twitter.com/realchrisrufo/status/1413966764463902721 ?lang=en

6 https://twitchy.com/samj-3930/2021/07/11/literally-racist-liz -wheeler-wipes-the-floor-with-marc-lamont-hill-for-his-com ments-on-all-white-people-being-racist-watch/

7 John McWhorter, linguist and CRT critic, offers examples of "religious anti-racism": the resignation of curator Gary Garrels from the San Francisco Museum of Modern Art for using the term "reverse racism"; and the *New York Times* suspending

Alison Roman's food column because she criticized two women celebrities of color. In both cases, McWhorter reduces the larger, underlying, and complicating considerations to the more superficial reading of stand-alone events. Morning Edition, "'Woke racism': John McWhorter argues against what he calls a religion of anti-racism," NPR, November 26, 2021. https://www.npr.org/2021/11/05/1052650979/mcwhorters-new-book-woke-racism-attacks-leading-thinkers-on-race

8 Henry A. Giroux, "Rewriting the discourse of racial identity towards a pedagogy and politics of whiteness," *Harvard Educational Review*, 67, 2. Summer 1997. https://www.hepg.org/her-home/issues/harvard-educational-review-volume-67-issue-2/herarticle/towards-a-pedagogy-and-politics-of-whiteness_226

9 Consider in France, "Le 'décolonialisme,' une stratégie hégémonique: l'appel de 80 intellectuels," *Le Point*, November 28, 2018 (modified July 17, 2020). https://www.lepoint.fr/politique/le-decolonialisme-une-strategie-hegemonique-l-appel-de-80-intellectuels-28-11-2018-2275104_20.php

   And in Germany, the controversies that swirled around documenta 15. Cf. Ruangrupa, "Anti-semitism accusations against documenta: A scandal about a rumor," efflux, May 7, 2022. https://www.e-flux.com/notes/467337/diversity-as-a-threat-a-scandal-about-a-rumor

10 Norimitsu Onishi, "Will American ideas tear France apart? Some of its leaders think so," *New York Times*, February 9, 2021. https://www.nytimes.com/2021/02/09/world/europe/france-threat-american-universities.html

11 Isaac Stanley-Becker, "Inside a stealth 'persuasion machine' promising Republican victories in 2022," *Washington Post*, April 3, 2021.

12 U.S. Supreme Court, *Parents Involved in Community Schools vs. Seattle School District et al.*, US 551 (2007), pp. 40–41.

13 Russell Lewis, *Anti-Racism: A Mania Exposed.* Quartet Books, 1988

14 Rachel Scully, "Texas state House Speaker bans the word 'racism' amid voting bill debate," *The Hill*, August 27, 2021.

15 The classic study is by Marc Mauer and Tracy Huling, "Young Black Americans and the criminal justice system: Five years later," The Sentencing Project, October 1995. https://www.sen tencingproject.org/wp-content/uploads/2016/01/Young-Black -Americans-and-the-Criminal-Justice-System-Five-Years-Later .pdf

For an updated analysis, see The U.S.A. Sentencing Commission, "Demographic differences in sentencing," November 14, 2017. https://www.ussc.gov/research/research-reports/demographic -differences-sentencing

16 Michael J. Sandel, *The Tyranny of Merit: What's Become of the Common Good?* Farrar, Strauss, Giroux, 2020. Cf. Lani Guinier, *The Tyranny of the Meritocracy: Democratizing Higher Education in America.* Penguin, 2016.

17 Carly Roman, "Josh Hawley proposes anti-critical race theory 'Love America Act'," *Washington Examiner*, July 24, 2021. https://www.washingtonexaminer.com/news/josh-hawley-pro poses-anti-critical-race-theory-love-america-act

18 Carly Roman, "Tom Cotton creates investigation into critical race theory training at Raytheon," *Washington Examiner*, July 13, 2021. https://www.washingtonexaminer.com/news/tom-cot ton-critical-race-theory-raytheon

19 Ibram X. Kendi, "Pass an anti-racist constitutional amendment," *Politico.com.* https://www.politico.com/interactives/2019/how -to-fix-politics-in-america/inequality/pass-an-anti-racist-consti tutional-amendment/

20 Ta-Nehisi Coates, "The case for reparations," *The Atlantic*, June 2014. https://www.theatlantic.com/magazine/archive/2014/06 /the-case-for-reparations/361631/

Olufemi Táíwò, *Reconsidering Reparations.* Oxford University Press, 2021. Katherine Franke, *Repair: Redeeming the Promise of Abolition.* Haymarket Books, 2019.

21 Ibram X. Kendi, *How to Be an Antiracist.* Penguin, 2019.

22 https://twitter.com/ConceptualJames/status/144592211991789
    9777/photo/1

9 Deregulating Racism

1 UCLA Civil Rights Project, "UCLA report finds changing U.S.
    demographics transform school segregation landscape 60 years
    after Brown v Board of Education," May 15, 2014. https://civil
    rightsproject.ucla.edu/news/press-releases/2014-press-releases
    /ucla-report-finds-changing-u.s.-demographics-transform-scho
    ol-segregation-landscape-60-years-after-brown-v-board-of-edu
    cation

2 In Europe, where immigration, especially from the Middle East,
    North and Sub-Saharan Africa, had a more visible presence
    and impact, anti-immigrant movements like the youth-driven
    Generation Identitaire and politicians like Viktor Orbán emerged.

3 Hill holds a distinguished professorship in philosophy at a
    Catholic university. He is a member of "1776 Unites," the pro-
    Trufist association of Black conservative intellectuals.
        Patricia Williams, *The Alchemy of Race and Rights: Diary
    of a Law Professor*. Harvard University Press, 1992. Jason Hill,
    "Critical race theory aims to murder the souls of white children,"
    The Federalist, August 13, 2021. https://thefederalist.com/2021
    /08/13/critical-race-theory-aims-to-murder-the-souls-of-white
    -children/

4 Cf. Elizabeth Lasch-Quinn, *Racial Experts: How Racial Etiquette,
    Sensitivity Training, and New Age Therapy Hijacked the Civil
    Rights Revolution*. Rowman and Littlefield, 2002.

5 Robin DiAngelo, *Nice Racism: How Progressive White People
    Perpetuate Racial Harm*. Penguin Random House, 2021.

6 ConceptualJames likewise has a litany of such terms on his
    website, and has self-published a book mimicking the Rufoistic
    talking points that CRT is dressed-up Marxism. James Lindsay,
    Race Marxism. Independently published, 2022. For his website,
    see https://newdiscourses.com/translations-from-the-wokish/

7 In 2011, Anders Breivik, renowned for his anti-Islamic and anti-

feminist views, murdered eight people in Oslo and then shot dead sixty-nine mostly young participants attending a Workers Youth League summer camp on the Norwegian island of Utøya.

8 Jonathan Butcher, *Splintered: Critical Race Theory and the Progressive War on Truth*. Bombardier Books, 2022.

9 Stephanie Saul, "A college fights 'leftist academics' by expanding into charter schools," *New York Times*, April 10, 2022. https:// www.nytimes.com/2022/04/10/us/hillsdale-college-charter-sch ools.html?referringSource=articleShare&fbclid=IwAR3eQmOR XKUdT2qNR69rQyo-VerS9sOlV2_V9aL-b7ghcRPOSOCWwat 2jXo

10 Robert Coles, *The Story of Ruby Bridges*. Scholastic, 2010.

11 A mother of a private-school child in a Virginia suburb started a campaign targeting the public school in her district also for allowing the Ruby Bridges book to be taught. Two school-board affiliates in Virginia Beach, one of whom declares herself a "woke-ness and critical race theory checker," have requested that the district Superintendent ban from district high-school curricula and libraries six books because of the sexual content, including Nobel Laureate Toni Morrison's novel, *The Bluest Eye*, and the comic book inspired by John Lewis, *Good Trouble: Lessons from the Civil Rights Handbook*. The wokeness checker said she was "disgusted and disturbed" by the "first few pages" of Morrison's classic and, without reading more, that it was inappropriate for seventeen- and eighteen-year-olds. "Good trouble," apparently, is too much trouble because racially challenging.

Brendan Morrow, "Anti-critical race theory parents reportedly object to teaching Ruby Bridges book," *Yahoo!News*, July 8, 2021. https://www.yahoo.com/news/anti-critical-race-theory-parents -135510393.html; Gabriella Borter, "'Critical race theory' roils a Tennessee school district," *Reuters*, September 21, 2021. https:// www.yahoo.com/news/critical-race-theory-roils-tennessee-160 808609.html

12 https://www.pbs.org/video/african-americans-many-rivers-cross -ruby-bridges-desegregates-school/

13 John Haltiwanger, "More than 4-in-10 Republicans don't want schools teaching the history of racism whatsoever: New poll," *Business Insider*, November 10, 2021.

14 Liz Mineo, "How textbooks taught white supremacy," *Harvard Gazette*, September 4, 2020. https://news.harvard.edu/gazette /story/2020/09/harvard-historian-examines-how-textbooks-tau ght-white-supremacy/?fbclid=IwAR0QOkdGfhREqueHQs2GnI KxriEYflIMAw2I9W3KBEniYrCNgtuFSVe4Dyc

15 Schools in European states long taught the history of colonialism and slavery as part of their country's "civilizing mission." In the last decade more or less, with variations across states, schools in Britain, France, Germany, now in the Netherlands, and even Belgium have increasingly turned to providing a more honest and accurate understanding of their country's "uncomfortable" role in colonialism and the slave trade.

16 Hannah Natanson, "It started with a mock 'slave trade' and a school resolution against racism," *Washington Post*, July 24, 2021. https://www.washingtonpost.com/local/education/mock -slave-trade-critical-race-theory/2021/07/23/b4372c36-e9a8-11 eb-ba5d-55d3b5ffcaf1_story.html

17 https://freetolearn.org/

18 https://twitter.com/SenTomCotton/status/144520310328073 4209

19 https://www.foxnews.com/politics/department-of-justice-garla nd-school-boards-crt-threats

20 Tyler O'Neill, "FBI conducting 'intersectionality' training for employees," Fox News, October 7, 2021. https://www.yahoo .com/news/fbi-conducting-apos-intersectionality-apos-1013510 69.html

21 Cf. Adam Serwer, *The Cruelty is the Point: The Past, Present, and Future of Trump's America*. Penguin Random House, 2022.

22 Martin Pengelly, "Fresh calls for Fox News to fire Tucker Carlson over 'replacement theory'," *Guardian*, September 25, 2021. https://www.theguardian.com/media/2021/sep/25/tucker-carls on-fox-news-anti-defamation-league

23 Anita Snow, "1 in 3 fears immigrants influence US elections: AP-Norc poll," *Associated Press*, May 9, 2022. NORC is a highly regarded independent, bipartisan research group based at the University of Chicago. https://apnews.com/article/immigration -2022-midterm-elections-covid-health-media-2ebbd3849ca35e c76f0f91120639d9d4

24 Mike Hixenbough and Antonia Hylton, "Southlake," NBCNews Podcast, https://www.nbcnews.com/southlake-podcast

25 Cf. Alan Feuer, "Fears of white people losing out permeate Capitol rioters' towns, study finds," *New York Times*, April 6, 2021. https://www.nytimes.com/2021/04/06/us/politics/capitol -riot-study.html

26 Dana Milbank, "A hero of the Trump right shows his true colors: Whites only," *Washington Post*, July 27. https://www.washing tonpost.com/opinions/2022/07/27/viktor-orban-cpac-conserv atives-welcome-racism/

27 Mike Hixenbaugh, "How a far-right, Christian cellphone company 'took over' four Texas school boards," NBC News, August 25, 2022. https://www.nbcnews.com/news/us-news/-christian -cell-company-patriot-mobile-took-four-texas-school-boards -rcna44583

28 https://centerforpolitics.org/crystalball/articles/project-home -fire-center-for-politics-research-reveals-outsized-role-immigr ation-plays-in-fueling-our-national-divide/

29 Glenn Ellmers,"'Conservativism' is no longer enough," *The American Mind: A Publication of the Claremont Institute*, March 24, 2022. https://americanmind.org/salvo/why-the-claremont -institute-is-not-conservative-and-you-shouldnt-be-either/

30 Senator Ted Cruz, "Critical race theory: A lecture," Leadership Institute, December 2021. https://secured.leadershipinstitute.org /cruz-crt

31 1776 Unites is headed by a former Ben Carson staffer and Carson's son is a board member. Carson served as Donald Trump's Secretary of Housing and Urban Development.

32 Aisha Powell, "Bernice King, MLK's daughter, called race profi-

teer by GOP senate candidate," *the Grio*, September 25, 2021. https://www.yahoo.com/news/bernice-king-mlk-daughter-cal led-193608734.html

33 Cf. Marjorie Garber, *Character: The History of a Cultural Expression*. Farrar, Strauss and Giroux, 2020.

34 James Barragán, Abby Livingston, and Carla Astudillo, "Texas reduces Black and Hispanic majority congressional districts in proposed map, despite people of color fueling population growth," *The Texas Tribune*, September 27, 2021. https://www .texastribune.org/2021/09/24/texas-congressional-redistricting/

35 Hua Hsu, "The End of White America?" *The Atlantic*, January/ February 2009. https://www.theatlantic.com/magazine/archive /2009/01/the-end-of-white-america/307208/

36 Isaiah Berlin, "Two concepts of liberty," 31 October, 1958. https://berlin.wolf.ox.ac.uk/published_works/tcl/tcl-a.pdf

37 David Theo Goldberg, *The Threat of Race: Reflections on Racial Neoliberalism*. Wiley-Blackwell, 2009.

38 Elizabeth Anker, *Ugly Freedoms*. Duke University Press, 2022.

39 Consider here Alana Lentin's account of "frozen racism." Lentin, *Why Race Still Matters*. Polity Press, 2020.

10 Executing Critical Race Theory

1 Jon McWhorter, *Woke Racism: How a New Religion has Betrayed Black America*. Penguin, 2021.

2 Tom Klingenstein, "Trump's virtues," July 6, 2022. https://www .youtube.com/watch?v=R-GAw1lLWJA

3 California Department of Education 2022 Revision of the Mathematics Framework. https://www.cde.ca.gov/ci/ma/cf/in dex.asp?te=1&nl=john-mcwhorter&emc=edit_jm_20211111

4 John McWhorter, "Let's not kid ourselves. Some schools teach critical race theory lite," *New York Times*, November 9, 2021.

5 Critics of self-declared "anti-racist math teaching" in schools often confuse advocating for anti-racist teaching practices with "anti-racist mathematics," whatever the latter might mean. This

confusion might be helped along by sometimes unfortunate advocate language like "ethnomathematics" or lists of terms deemed "white supremacist" – objectivity, perfectionism, etc., which can just as easily be used with no racial connotation. Cf. *A Pathway to Equitable Math Instruction: Dismantling Racism in Mathematics Instruction.* May 2021. https://equitablemath.org/wp-content/uploads/sites/2/2020/11/1_STRIDE1.pdf

6 Brooke Leigh Howard, "Beloved black principal fired in ludicrous critical race theory spat," *The Daily Beast*, September 22, 2021. https://www.thedailybeast.com/grapevine-colleyville-texas-school-board-ousts-black-principal-james-whitfield-over-critical-race-theory

7 Khiara Bridges, *Critical Race Theory: A Primer.* Foundation Press, 2018.

8 Christopher R. Rufo, "Don't be evil," *City Journal*, September 8, 2021. https://www.city-journal.org/a-radical-racial-reeducation-program-at-google

9 Lauren Berlant, *Cruel Optimism.* Duke University Press, 2011.

10 Tom Simonite, "What really happened when Google Ousted Timnit Gebru?" *Wired*, June 8, 2021. https://www.wired.com/story/google-timnit-gebru-ai-what-really-happened/

11 April Glaser, "Current and ex-employees allege Google drastically rolled back diversity and inclusion programs," *NBCNews*, April 13, 2021. https://www.nbcnews.com/news/us-news/current-ex-employees-allege-google-drastically-rolled-back-diversity-inclusion-n1206181

12 ACT Bible: "Anti-critical race theory translation." Dyer advertised the spoof translation, with enticing examples, on a dedicated website, adding a "Buy Now" button. Clicking the button brought one to Amy Grant's "Baby, Baby" music video. His point made about the pitfalls of living in fear, here of anti-racist theory, Dyer let the website lapse. Dale Chamberlain, "Satirical 'Anti-critical theory' Bible translation takes aim at 'colorblind' theology," *Church Leaders*, December 9, 2021. https://churchleaders.com/news/412278-act-bible-john-dyer.html

13 Brian Lopez, "Texas House committee to investigate school districts' books on race and sexuality," *Texas Tribune*, October 26, 2021. https://www.texastribune.org/2021/10/26/texas-scho ol-books-race-sexuality/
      The book list: https://static.texastribune.org/media/files/94fee 7ff93eff9609f141433e41f8ae1/krausebooklist.pdf

14 Timothy Bella, "DeSantis invokes MLK as he promotes Stop Woke Act against critical race theory," *Washington Post*, December 15, 2021. https://www.washingtonpost.com/politics /2021/12/15/desantis-stop-woke-act-mlk-crt/

15 Jennifer Berkshire and Jack Schneider, *The Wolf at the Door: The Dismantling of Public Education and the Future of School*. The New Press, 2020.

16 Luke Winkie, "US conservative parents push for book bans – and unintentionally make reading cool again," *Guardian*, December 21, 2021. https://www.theguardian.com/education/2021/dec/23 /us-book-bans-conservative-parents-reading

17 https://law.ucla.edu/academics/centers/critical-race-studies/uc la-law-crt-forward-tracking-project

18 Gloria Wekker, *White Innocence: Paradoxes of Colonialism and Race*. Duke University Press, 2016.

19 Alison Flood, "Sharp rise in parents seeking to ban anti-racist books in US schools," *Guardian*, April 6, 2021.

20 Bosley Crowther, "The Screen: Minstrel show 'Othello': Radical makeup marks Olivier's interpretation," *New York Times*, February 2, 1966. https://www.nytimes.com/1966/02/02/arch ives/the-screen-minstrel-show-othelloradical-makeup-marks -oliviers.html
      Jennifer Schuessler, "A blackface 'Othello' shocks, and a professor steps back from class," *New York Times*, October 15, 2021. https://www.nytimes.com/2021/10/15/arts/music/othello-black face-bright-sheng.html

21 Eyal Weizman, "Open verification," e-flux Architecture, June 2019. https://www.e-flux.com/architecture/becoming-digital/24 8062/open-verification/

22 Duncan Pritchard, "Why curiosity, integrity, humility and tenacity contribute to the good life," The UCI Podcast, June 3, 2021. I owe the reference to my good friend and colleague, Aaron James. https://www.stitcher.com/show/the-uci-podcast/episode/why -curiosity-integrity-humility-and-tenacity-contribute-to-the-go od-life-84454675

23 For a recent example of this, see Ayaan Hirsi Ali, "Critical theory's new disguise," UnHerd.com, October 7, 2021. https:// unherd.com/2021/10/critical-race-theorys-new-disguise/

24 Harry Frankfurt, *On Bullshit*. Princeton University Press, 2005, p. 61.

25 Martin Luther King, "Proud to be maladjusted," UCLA, April 27, 1965. https://www.youtube.com/watch?v=t2vD1skiz80

26 James Baldwin, "Stranger in the village," in *Notes of a Native Son*. Beacon, 1955. The essay first appeared in *Harper's Magazine* in 1953.

Index